face2face

Upper Intermediate Workbook with Key

SECOND EDITION

Nicholas Tims & Jan Bell
with Chris Redston & Gillie Cunningham

CAMBRIDGE UNIVERSITY PRESS

CAMBRIDGE UNIVERSITY PRESS
Cambridge, New York, Melbourne, Madrid, Cape Town,
Singapore, São Paulo, Delhi, Mexico City

Cambridge University Press
The Edinburgh Building, Cambridge CB2 8RU, UK

www.cambridge.org
Information on this title: www.cambridge.org/9781107609563

© Cambridge University Press 2013

This publication is in copyright. Subject to statutory exception
and to the provisions of relevant collective licensing agreements,
no reproduction of any part may take place without the written
permission of Cambridge University Press.

First published 2013

Printed in Italy by L.E.G.O. S.p.A.

A catalogue record for this publication is available from the British Library

ISBN 978-1-107-60956-3 Workbook with Key
ISBN 978-1-107-60957-0 Workbook without Key
ISBN 978-1-107-42201-8 Student's Book with DVD-ROM
ISBN 978-1-107-62935-6 Teacher's Book with DVD
ISBN 978-1-107-42203-2 Class Audio CDs (3)

Cambridge University Press has no responsibility for the persistence or
accuracy of URLs for external or third-party internet websites referred to in
this publication, and does not guarantee that any content on such websites is,
or will remain, accurate or appropriate. Information regarding prices, travel
timetables and other factual information given in this work is correct at
the time of first printing but Cambridge University Press does not guarantee
the accuracy of such information thereafter.

Contents

Vocabulary	Grammar and Real World	Reading and Writing
Lessons 1A–D p5		**Portfolio 1 p64**
VOCABULARY Language ability; Education; Verb patterns (1)	GRAMMAR The English verb system; Auxiliaries in verb forms; Other uses of auxiliaries REAL WORLD Keeping a conversation going	**Planning and drafting** Reading an article about learning languages Writing planning and drafting an article
Lessons 2A–D p10		**Portfolio 2 p66**
VOCABULARY Expressing frequency; Feelings and opinions; Word building (1): suffixes	GRAMMAR Present and past habits, repeated actions and states; *be used to*, *get used to* REAL WORLD Discussion language (1): agreeing and disagreeing politely	**Letters to a newspaper** Reading two letters to a newspaper Writing giving emphasis
Lessons 3A–D p15		**Portfolio 3 p68**
VOCABULARY Crime; Criminals and crime verbs; Crime and punishment; Verbs and prepositions	GRAMMAR Second conditional; alternatives for *if*; Third conditional REAL WORLD Making, refusing and accepting offers	**Advice leaflets** Reading a police leaflet about personal safety Writing leaflets: giving advice
Lessons 4A–D p20		**Portfolio 4 p70**
VOCABULARY Phrasal verbs (1); Books and reading; Connecting words: reason and contrast; Ways of exaggerating	GRAMMAR Narrative verb forms; Past Perfect Continuous; Defining, non-defining and reduced relative clauses REAL WORLD Saying you're surprised or not surprised	**A biography** Reading a biography of Johnny Depp Writing a short biography: avoiding repetition; adding detail and personal comment
Lessons 5A–D p25		**Portfolio 5 p72**
VOCABULARY Adjectives (1); Phrasal verbs (2); Guessing meaning from context; Adjectives for giving opinions	GRAMMAR Ways of comparing; Future verb forms; Future Continuous REAL WORLD Discussion language (2): opinions	**Preparing a presentation** Reading a science presentation Writing the language of presentations
Lessons 6A–D p30		**Portfolio 6 p74**
VOCABULARY Phrases with *take*; Compound adjectives describing character; Back referencing	GRAMMAR Uses of verb+*ing*; Modal verbs (1); levels of certainty about the future REAL WORLD Polite interruptions	**Describing a place you love** Reading a description of a place Writing describing places: reduced relative clauses, strong adjectives
Lessons 7A–D p35		**Portfolio 7 p76**
VOCABULARY State verbs; Business and trade; Word building (2): prefixes; On the phone	GRAMMAR Simple and continuous aspects; activity and state verbs; Present Perfect Simple and Present Perfect Continuous REAL WORLD Problems on the phone	**Including relevant information** Reading a leaflet, an article, an email, notes and a fundraising letter Writing semi-formal letters/emails: including relevant information
Lessons 8A–D p40		**Portfolio 8 p78**
VOCABULARY Dealing with money; Phrasal verbs (3): money; Synonyms	GRAMMAR Wishes (1): *I hope ...*; *It's time ...*; Wishes (2): *should have* REAL WORLD Apologising	**Reporting facts** Reading an article reporting on consumer spending Writing generalising; giving examples
Answer Key pi–viii		
Lessons 9A–D p45		**Portfolio 9 p80**
VOCABULARY The cinema; Entertainment adjectives; Homonyms	GRAMMAR The passive; *as*, *like*, *such as*, *so*, *such* REAL WORLD Making and responding to suggestions	**Website reviews** Reading a review of two websites Writing reviews: beginning reviews, useful phrases
Lessons 10A–D p50		**Portfolio 10 p82**
VOCABULARY Household jobs; Adjectives for views and behaviour; Compound nouns and adjectives	GRAMMAR *have/get something done*, *get someone to do something*, *do something yourself*; Quantifiers REAL WORLD Adding emphasis	**A discursive article** Reading an article about combining parenthood and careers Writing a discursive article: common connecting words
Lessons 11A–D p55		**Portfolio 11 p84**
VOCABULARY Work collocations; Business collocations; Verb patterns (2): reporting verbs; Advertising	GRAMMAR Describing future events; Future Perfect; Reported speech REAL WORLD Discussion language (3)	**Formal and informal emails** Reading two emails asking for and giving information Writing making arrangements in informal and more formal emails
Lessons 12A–C p60		**Portfolio 12 p86**
VOCABULARY Colloquial words/phrases; Vague language expressions; Idioms	GRAMMAR Modal verbs (2): deduction in the present and the past; Past forms of modals and related verbs	**A personal email** Reading a personal email about a ghostly experience Writing a personal email about an experience: common mistakes
	Upper Intermediate Reading and Writing Progress Portfolio p88	

Acknowledgements

The authors would like to thank all those involved in *face2face* for all their work, in particular Greg Sibley (Managing Editor), Andrew Reid (freelance editor) and Chris Williams (Production Controller) for their invaluable editorial and production skills. Thanks also to Chris Redston and Gillie Cunningham for their support and advice.

Nicholas Tims would also like to thank Clare Turnbull for her patience, encouragement and inspiration.

Jan Bell would like to thank Bruce, Alex and Lucy for their support.

The authors and publishers are grateful to the following contributors:
Blooberry Design Ltd: text design and page make-up
Hilary Luckcock: picture research

The authors and publishers acknowledge the following sources of copyright material and are grateful for the permissions granted. While every effort has been made, it has not always been possible to identify the sources of all the material used, or to trace all copyright holders. If any omissions are brought to our notice, we will be happy to include the appropriate acknowledgements on reprinting.

BBC Wildlife for the text on p. 28 'Pigeon fanciers' originally published in *BBC Wildlife Magazine*, December 2009 © Immediate Media Company Limited Bristol © Author: Andy Allen; Guardian News & Media Ltd for the text on p. 33 adapted from 'School uniform does not improve results – discuss' by Stephen Northern, *The Guardian*, 18.01.11. Copyright © Guardian News & Media Ltd 2011.

The publishers are grateful to the following for permission to reproduce copyright photographs and material:
Key: l = left, c = centre, r = right, t = top, b = bottom
The authors and publishers acknowledge the following sources of copyright material and are grateful for the permissions granted. While every effort has been made, it has not always been possible to identify the sources of all the material used, or to trace all copyright holders. If any omissions are brought to our notice, we will be happy to include the appropriate acknowledgements on reprinting.

The publisher has used its best endeavours to ensure that the URLs for external websites referred to in this book are correct and active at the time of going to press. However, the publisher has no responsibility for the websites and can make no guarantee that a site will remain live or that the content is or will remain appropriate.

p5(T): Punchstock/Pixland; p5(C): Alamy BlueMoon Stock; p5(B): Shutterstock/NorthGeorgia Media; p7: Getty Images/Monkey Business Images; p10: Travel Library/Philip Enticknap; p12: Corbis/Ocean; p13: Masterfile; p14: Getty Images/Photodisc; p16: Getty Images Entertainment Pool; p18(both): Shutterstock/Ecelop; p22: Masterfile/Jon Feingersh; p23: Rex Features; p24: Alamy/Profimedia International s.r.o.; p25: Photolibrary/Animals Animals/Earthscene; p27: Alamy/Goss Images; p28: Thinkstock/David De Lossy; p31: Getty Images/Image Source; p32: Shutterstock/Cindy Hughes; p33: Guardian/Fabio De Paola; p34: Superstock/Age Fotostock; p35(T): Corbis/Bettmann; p35(B): Rex Features/Everett Collection; p40(TL): Thinkstock/istockphoto; p42(T): Shutterstock/Creatista; p42(B): Alamy/Image Source; p44: Rex Features; p45(L): Punchstock/Brand X; p45(R): The Kobal Collection/Film 4/Celador Films/Pathe International; p47: Thinkstock/Stockbyte; p48: imagesandstories.com; p49: istockphoto/kevinruss; p50: istockphoto/sturti; p51(TL): Shutterstock/Monkey Business Images; p51(CL): istockphoto/Squaredpixels; p51(BL): istockphoto/c glade; p51(TR): Getty Images/Thinkstock Images; p51(BR): Fotolia/Rido; p52(T): Corbis/Ronnie Kaufman; p52(B): Alamy/Ace Stock Ltd; p53: Punchstock/Photodisc; p54: Corbis/John Bower/Loop Images; p55: Thinkstock/Stockbyte; p56: Alamy/Mike Watson Images; p57: Thinkstock/istockphoto; p61: Alamy/JTB Communications Inc; p64: Corbis/Bloomimage; p66: Corbis/Stockbyte; p68: Getty Images/Taxi; p70: Getty Images Entertainment/Chris Jackson; p72: Alamy/amana images inc; p74(T): Alamy/PCL; p74(B): Photolibrary/ Angel M Fitor.

Realia images: p8(gears): Thinkstock/istockphoto; p33(A+ grade): Thinkstock/istockphoto; p56(rings): Thinkstock/Thomas Northcut; p76(bicycle): Thinkstock/istockphoto; p76(UK map): Thinkstock/Zoonar.

Front cover photos by: Corbis/Steve Hix/Somos Images (BL); Glowimages (TC, TCR, UCR); Shutterstock/Yuri Arcurs (TL, TR); Shutterstock/Andresr (TCL, BCR); Shutterstock/Monkey Business Images (UC); Shutterstock/Elena Elisseeva (LCL); Shutterstock/Konstantin Sutyagin (BR); Thinkstock/Thomas Northcut (UCL); Thinkstock/Chris Clinton (LC); Thinkstock/Jupiterimages (BCL); Thinkstock/Stockbyte (BC).

The publishers would like to thank the following illustrators:
Fred Blunt, Inigo Montoya (c/o Dirty Vectors), Mark Duffin, Graham Kennedy, Joanne Kerr (c/o New Division), NAF (c/o Meiklejohn Illustration Agency), Lucy Truman (c/o New Division).

Corpus
Development of this publication has made use of the Cambridge English Corpus (CEC). The CEC is a computer database of contemporary spoken and written English, which currently stands at over one billion words. It includes British English, American English and other varieties of English. It also includes the Cambridge Learner Corpus, developed in collaboration with the University of Cambridge ESOL Examinations. Cambridge University Press has built up the CEC to provide evidence about language use that helps to produce better language teaching materials.

English Profile
This product is informed by the English Vocabulary Profile, built as part of English Profile, a collaborative programme designed to enhance the learning, teaching and assessment of English worldwide. Its main funding partners are Cambridge University Press and Cambridge ESOL and its aim is to create a 'profile' for English linked to the Common European Framework of Reference for Languages (CEFR). English Profile outcomes, such as the English Vocabulary Profile, will provide detailed information about the language that learners can be expected to demonstrate at each CEFR level, offering a clear benchmark for learners' proficiency. For more information, please visit www.englishprofile.org

1A A global language
Language Summary 1, Student's Book p127

Language ability VOCABULARY 1.1

1 Read what Carl, Heidi and Maria say about speaking languages. Fill in the gaps with the phrases in the boxes.

| ~~bad at~~ | can't speak a word | know a few words |

To be honest, I'm quite ^{1} _bad at_ languages.
I ^{2}_____ of French that I learned at school, but I ^{3}_____ of anything else.

Carl

| can also get by | 'm reasonably good | picked up |

My first language is Swiss German, but I live near the border, so I ^{4}_____ at Italian.
I ^{5}_____ in French. We went to Lyon last summer and I ^{6}_____ the language very quickly.

Heidi

| also fluent in | can have a conversation |
| 'm bilingual | it's a bit rusty |

My mother is Spanish and my father is French so I ^{7}_____. I'm ^{8}_____ English, which I need for work. I ^{9}_____ in German, but ^{10}_____.

Maria

2 Rewrite these sentences using the words/phrases in brackets.

1 I don't know any Japanese. (word)
   I can't speak a word of Japanese.

2 I speak enough German for holidays. (get by)
   I _____ on holiday.

3 My sister can speak Chinese very well. (fluent)
   My _____

4 I haven't spoken Portuguese for a long time. (bit rusty)
   My _____

5 I learned a few words of Italian on holiday. (picked)
   I _____

6 I can speak both Turkish and Spanish perfectly. (bilingual)
   I'm _____

The English verb system GRAMMAR 1.1

3 a Match sentence beginnings 1–9 to endings a–i.

1 In the year 1000, English   _b_
2 The English language was   ___
3 A hundred years ago, many people were   ___
4 Cambridge University Press has   ___
5 By the 21st century, English had   ___
6 Immigration, new technologies, popular culture and even war have   ___
7 At present, over a billion people are   ___
8 English is   ___
9 However, more people speak   ___

a now learning English worldwide.
b had approximately 40,000 words.
c all contributed to the growth of English.
d using French as an international language.
e grown to over 500,000 words.
f been publishing English-language teaching books since 1975.
g Mandarin Chinese than any other language.
h taken to North America by settlers in the 17th century.
i used as a first language in at least 75 countries.

b Match sentences 1–9 in **3a** to these verb forms.

Present Simple   _9_
Present Continuous   ___
Present Simple passive   ___
Present Perfect Simple   ___
Present Perfect Continuous   ___
Past Simple   ___
Past Continuous   ___
Past Simple passive   ___
Past Perfect Simple   ___

4 **a** Read the first part of an article about 'Basic English' and choose the correct verb forms.

b Read the second part of the article below and fill in the gaps with the correct form of the verbs in brackets.

The idea of inventing an international language is not a new one. Over the past 180 years, linguists ¹*have created*/ *created* over ten different languages that ²*are based/be based* on German, Spanish, English and even musical notes. One of the most influential of these ³*had been/was* 'Basic English'.

By 1923, the First World War ⁴*was/had been* over for five years, but Europe was still ⁵*recovering/recovered* from its effects. Charles Kay Ogden, a linguist and writer, was running several bookshops in Cambridge. He ⁶*had just written/just written* published a book which described how we use language. The success of his book ⁷*has inspired/inspired* Ogden to design a universal language – one that was much simpler than English, but ⁸*doesn't/didn't* require native English speakers to study a different language. In 1930, Ogden's book *Basic English: A General Introduction with Rules and Grammar* ⁹*was/were* published.

It is estimated that, on average, it ¹⁰*takes/took* about seven years to become fluent in English. Ogden ¹¹*believed/was believing* that 'Basic English' could be learned in seven weeks. There ¹²*had been/were* only 850 words, and the grammar was simplified with very few exceptions to each rule.

The language ¹ *attracted* (attract) the attention of educators all over the world, but its development ² _____ (interrupt) by the Second World War. After the war, both the British prime minister and the president of the United States ³_____ (look) for ideas that might promote world peace. They both ⁴_____ (give) speeches that supported the use of Basic English. In the past 60 years, the language ⁵_____ (have) some success. In some parts of East Asia, teachers ⁶_____ (still; use) Ogden's word lists. However, in the main, the language has disappeared.

Now that we ⁷_____ (know) that there are many more non-native than native speakers of English, some linguists ⁸_____ (recently; ask) whether we should revisit Ogden's ideas. There is even a version of the Wikipedia website which ⁹_____ (write) in 'Basic English' for non-native learners of the language. Google it now!

1B Open learning

Education VOCABULARY 1.2

1 Complete the crossword with words connected with education.

1 money given by an organisation to pay for someone's studies (11)
2 a talk on an academic subject, especially at university (7)
3 a long piece of writing on a particular subject, especially one that is done as part of a course at college or university (12)
4 money that students must pay to universities for their courses (4)
5 an agreement by which a student at a college or university borrows money from a bank to pay for their education and then pays the money back after they finish studying and start a job (7, 4)
6 a class, especially at university, with a few students (8)
7 an advanced degree, usually lasting for one year (7)
8 someone who is studying for their first degree at university (13)
9 a student who has already got one degree and is studying at a university for a more advanced qualification (12)
10 a senior person who teaches at a British university (9)

Auxiliaries in verb forms GRAMMAR 1.2
Other uses of auxiliaries GRAMMAR 1.3

2 a Are sentences 1–8 correct? Change the incorrect sentences.

       is
1 Everyone here ~~are~~ doing a Master's degree.
2 Did you went to the seminar yesterday?
3 I do work very hard, but I still find the course difficult.
4 Some universities does give scholarships, but we don't.
5 I'm the only person here who went to a state school, aren't I?
6 If I were you, I don't eat in the college canteen.
7 You like doing exams or prefer continuous assessment?
8 I've be invited to apply for a PhD, but the fees are too high.

b Match the correct and corrected sentences in **2a** to replies a–h.

a _4_ Don't you?   e ___ They are, aren't they?
b ___ Well, I'm not.   f ___ Are you?
c ___ I don't enjoy either!   g ___ So do I.
d ___ Wouldn't you? Why not?   h ___ No, I didn't.

3 Read the conversation and choose the correct auxiliary verb.

PHIL Hi. It's Sara, ¹ _isn't_ it? We met last week, ² _____ we?
SARA Yes, we ³ _____ . You're Phil.
PHIL Well remembered! You ⁴ _____ warn me when we met that you often forget names.
SARA I ⁵ _____ , unfortunately. But I ⁶ _____ making a special effort this week. Anyway, how ⁷ _____ it going?
PHIL OK. I ⁸ _____ already had a tutorial with my PhD tutor.
SARA ⁹ _____ you? Who's that?
PHIL His name's Professor Shavick. Everyone else was very impressed by him, but I ¹⁰ _____ . I ¹¹ _____ expect you know him.
SARA I ¹² _____ , actually. You see, I'm …
PHIL Oh, sorry, hold on – that's my phone ringing …

1	a	is	(b)	isn't	c	doesn't
2	a	didn't	b	haven't	c	aren't
3	a	did	b	do	c	have
4	a	have	b	do	c	did
5	a	'm	b	do	c	have
6	a	'm	b	've	c	'll
7	a	has	b	does	c	is
8	a	do	b	'd	c	've
9	a	Did	b	Have	c	Haven't
10	a	wasn't	b	didn't	c	haven't
11	a	'm not	b	don't	c	do
12	a	am	b	have	c	do

4 Read the second part of the conversation. Fill in the gaps with the correct positive or negative auxiliaries. Use contractions ('ve, 's, etc.) if possible.

PHIL Sorry, where were we? Yes, Professor Shavick. He's a bit strange, ¹ _isn't_ he? I ² _____ interviewed by him, so we hadn't met before.
SARA Neither ³ _____ I when I started here. And I must admit – he ⁴ _____ appear rather unusual when you first meet him.
PHIL Unusual? If I met him in the street, I ⁵ _____ probably run away screaming. All that hair! He's been spending far too much time with his computer. He should get out more often, ⁶ _____ he?
SARA Well, perhaps.
PHIL Anyway. I ⁷ _____ think I even asked you what you're doing your PhD in.
SARA Well, I ⁸ _____ not doing a PhD actually. I, er, teach here.
PHIL You don't, ⁹ _____ you?
SARA Er … yes. Computer science, as a matter of fact. Sorry, I ¹⁰ _____ going to say something earlier, but …
PHIL How embarrassing. So, Professor Shavick is a colleague of yours?
SARA Erm … well, I suppose he's my boss really. But ¹¹ _____ worry – I ¹² _____ tell him anything! And not all tutors are like him, I promise!

VOCABULARY 1C AND SKILLS

Getting results

Reading

1 Read the article quickly and choose the best definition of 'lateral thinking'.

'Lateral thinking' is …

a a new way of thinking about old problems.

b a fun way of solving puzzles.

c an alternative way of thinking about problems.

Verb patterns (1)

VOCABULARY 1.3

2 Read the article again. Fill in the gaps with the correct form of the verbs in brackets.

3 Read the article again. Which paragraph or paragraphs in the article:

1 encourage you not to give up thinking about the puzzle? _B_ , ___

2 tells you what you need to do if you want to use lateral thinking? ___

3 explains why some people are better at lateral thinking? ___

4 gives an example of solving a problem by lateral thinking? ___

5 presents a lateral-thinking problem for the reader to solve? ___

6 explains the way we traditionally deal with problems? ___

7 tells you where you can find the solution to the puzzle? ___

Teaching thinking

A Acting on an anonymous phone call, the police raid a house to arrest a suspected murderer. They don't know what he looks like but they know his name is John. Inside the house, they find a surgeon, a lorry driver, a mechanic and a fireman, all playing cards. Without hesitation or asking any questions, they arrest the fireman. How do they know the fireman is the murderer?

B The answer to the puzzle is printed at the bottom of the page. But if you don't know it, try [1] _not to look_ (not look) yet! Read this article and then force yourself [2]_____ (think) a little harder.

C In the 1960s, Edward de Bono, a Maltese doctor and writer, invented the phrase 'lateral thinking'. He believes that we understand the world by building up patterns based on experience. These patterns teach us [3]_____ (recognise) familiar problems and situations and allow us [4]_____ (make) simple decisions quickly. However, de Bono argues these patterns can also stop us from seeing the solution to a problem.

D Edward de Bono thinks that for every problem, you need [5]_____ (check) your assumptions. What did you assume when you read the puzzle above? To think laterally means you must avoid [6]_____ (make) assumptions about a problem and make yourself [7]_____ (think) 'outside the box'.

E Now think about the fireman puzzle again. Have you got the solution yet? No? Well, keep [8]_____ (read) then think again.

F Edward de Bono once asked some children [9]_____ (suggest) ways of estimating the height of a tall building. Some suggestions were asking the architect and also dropping a stone from the top, and measuring the time taken to fall. But one boy refused [10]_____ (take) the question seriously. "Put the building on its side and measure it," he said. The class laughed. Edward de Bono then managed [11]_____ (demonstrate) that this was actually a very sensible idea. You can measure the building, de Bono pointed out, in a photograph. And if you put something else in the photograph – that you know the height of – you can easily calculate the height of the building.

G In fact, children are often good at lateral thinking. With less life experience, they bring fewer assumptions to a problem, and so look for different solutions. So, if you can't answer the murderer puzzle yet, try asking a young person the same problem. You might [12]_____ (be) surprised at how simple they find it!

SOLUTION

The surgeon, lorry driver and mechanic were all women. The fireman was the only man.

1D REAL WORLD — Evening classes

Keeping a conversation going
REAL WORLD 1.1

1 a Choose the best response.

1. We'd like to do something more creative than yoga.
   a. What's it like?
   b. What sort of writing?
   (c). Like what, exactly?

2. I can't stand exams.
   a. Why's that?
   b. Such as?
   c. Don't you?

3. I'm doing a jewellery-making class at the moment.
   a. How do you mean?
   b. How's it going?
   c. Like what, exactly?

4. Richard wants to learn Chinese.
   a. In what way?
   b. How's it going?
   c. Does he?

b Match conversations 1–4 in **1a** to the next lines a–d.

a. _4_ Yes, he needs it for work.
b. ___ Bad memories from school, really.
c. ___ We're not sure. Maybe carpentry.
d. ___ Really well. I love it.

2 Complete conversations 1–5 with the correct question word and preposition.

| ~~Who~~ | What | How long | Who | Where |

| ~~with~~ | from | for | about | to |

1.
SAM Clare is starting her own business.
DAN Really? _Who with_ ?
SAM It's just her at the moment.

2.
PAUL Alex has written a screenplay.
KATE No way! _____ ?
PAUL It's a thriller, I think. But I don't know the story or anything.

3.
ROB We've got to give in our application forms soon.
AMY _____ ? Do you know?
ROB I think you can just leave them with the secretary.

4.
TIM I got this camera for less than half price.
CHRIS Did you? _____ ?
TIM On a website my brother told me about.

5.
SARA Our teacher's going away next week.
LUIS _____ ?
SARA Almost a fortnight, I think.

3 Fill in the gaps in the conversation. Use between one and three words.

JIM Clare! Hi!
CLARE Jim! What a coincidence. I was thinking about you recently.
JIM ¹ _Were_ you? Why ² _____ that?
CLARE I was wondering if you're still doing that jewellery class.
JIM No, I gave that up a few months ago.
CLARE ³ _____ come?
JIM Well, we moved house in March, so it's a bit far.
CLARE Really? ⁴ _____ to?
JIM Near here, actually. On Shelford Street. Anyway, ⁵ _____ going? Are you still teaching?
CLARE Yes, but not for much longer, thankfully.
JIM What ⁶ _____ mean?
CLARE Well, I'm starting my own training business.
JIM ⁷ _____ of training?
CLARE Presentations, mainly.
JIM You've always been good at that kind of thing, ⁸ _____ ? I guess teaching helps.
CLARE Absolutely. Anyway, enough about me. What's Shelford Street ⁹ _____ ?
JIM Great. It's a much bigger place than our old one. Of course, life is a little different these days.
CLARE Different? In ¹⁰ _____ ?
JIM Well, since we had the baby …
CLARE A baby? Congratulations! I had no idea!

Reading and Writing Portfolio 1 p64

2A It's bad for you!

Language Summary 2, Student's Book p130

Expressing frequency
VOCABULARY 2.1

1 a Read the nutritional advice in the 'Healthy eating' leaflet. Choose the correct phrases in these sentences.

1 You can eat chips (every so often)/most of the time.

2 Try to eat some fruit *once in a while/every day*.

3 It's alright to snack on biscuits *once in a while/most of the time*.

4 Only eat crisps *every now and again/more often than not*.

5 Eating red meat *most days/rarely* isn't good for you.

b Read these comments. Are the people following the advice in the leaflet? Write Y (Yes) or N (No).

1 [Y] More often than not I'll choose fish or chicken rather than a burger.

2 [ ] I have chips for dinner most days.

3 [ ] I seldom remember to eat an apple or an orange.

4 [ ] I have a biscuit with my coffee every now and again.

5 [ ] Every so often, when I'm on the computer, I'll have a packet of crisps.

6 [ ] I only eat vegetables at weekends.

7 [ ] My favourite food is cheese sandwiches on white bread – I eat them for lunch once in a while.

Healthy eating

✓ GO AHEAD! (EVERY DAY)
- fruit, nuts
- wholemeal bread
- white meat (e.g. chicken, turkey)
- vegetables
- white/oily fish

✗ BE CAREFUL! (ONCE A WEEK)
- crisps
- white bread, rice, pasta
- red meat
- fried or roast potatoes
- cakes, biscuits, chocolate

Present and past habits, repeated actions and states **GRAMMAR 2.1**

2 Choose the correct verb form. Sometimes both are possible.

When my father ¹(reached)/would reach 40, something strange ²*used to happen/happened* to him. Before this, he ³*was always eating/always used to eat* what he wanted, but now ⁴*he's never eating/he won't eat* any fried food and ⁵*he's always worrying/he worried* about how much sugar and salt there is in everything. This is the same man who ⁶*used to eat/would eat* chocolate all day long! These days ⁷*he gets up/he'd get up* early to go to the gym every morning before work. Before his 40th birthday, he ⁸*would even complain/was even complaining* about having to walk to the car!

3 Are the words/phrases in **bold** correct? Change the incorrect words/phrases and tick the correct phrases.

I used to live in a tiny village in southern Italy many years ago before I ¹**used to go** to university. At that time there ²**was** very little tourism so there ³**didn't use to be** many restaurants and there only ⁴**use to be** one small hotel. Because the village was so small everyone ⁵**would know** everyone else and so people ⁶**would always say** hello to you in the shops or while you were walking down the streets. We ⁷**spent** a lot of time sitting in cafés and bars, chatting to everyone in our bad Italian! It ⁸**would be** very cheap to eat out so we ate delicious food all the time for next to nothing. We ⁹**used to make** some fantastic friends and we still go back there from time to time to visit them.

1 _went_   4 _____   7 _____
2 ✓   5 _____   8 _____
3 _____ 6 _____   9 _____

4 Choose the correct endings.

1 My aunt is always apologising for everything she does.
   a) I find it really annoying!
   b She's very polite!
2 Fred used to like playing football
   a but he prefers watching it these days.
   b but he doesn't like watching it.
3 I went to Scotland for my holidays last year.
   a It would rain every day.
   b It rained every day.
4 I'll go out for a long walk when I'm feeling stressed.
   a It helps me clear my head.
   b It'd help me feel better.
5 My dad and I would watch *Match of the Day* together on television.
   a It used to be on at 10 p.m. on Saturdays.
   b I remember seeing it a couple of times.

5 Rewrite the sentences using the word in brackets.

1 I drank up to five cups of strong coffee every morning before I gave up. (would)
   I would drink up to five cups of strong coffee every morning before I gave up.
2 My doctor frequently tells me to take more exercise. (always)
3 My wife always checks the labels before she buys food. (will)
4 When I was a student, I was a vegetarian. (used to)
5 I never worried about my food until I put on weight. (used to)
6 When my children were small I never gave them fast food. (would)

2B Life's different here

Feelings and opinions VOCABULARY 2.2

1 Put sentences a–j in order 1–10.

a [1] I knew that Barcelona was famous
b [ ] Luckily they were more than satisfied
c [ ] of art and architecture, and were shocked
d [ ] of all the wonderful restaurants we went to while we were there.
e [ ] by the idea of sightseeing in the heat of the day.
f [ ] with the shopping in Barcelona, and I wasn't at all disappointed
g [ ] about the idea of visiting the cathedral and houses that Gaudí designed.
h [ ] by the fantastic buildings I saw. And none of us would ever get sick
i [ ] for its fantastic architecture so I was excited
j [ ] Unfortunately, however, the friends I went with were not very fond

2 Choose the correct prepositions.

Dear everyone,

Having a great time. Weather's fantastic so far. The kids seem fascinated ¹in/by how warm the sea is, although terrified ²of/at seeing a shark!

Thanks for the offer of a lift from the airport. Not sure yet ³about/at our plans, but will phone you soon to confirm. We aren't aware ⁴of/in any problems with the flights, anyway.

Hope you are impressed ⁵of/by the picture on the card. Josh chose it, of course!

Love,
Amanda

The Gill Family
132 Hart Road
Cambridge
CB9 3TY
UK

be used to, get used to GRAMMAR 2.2

3 Fill in the gaps with the correct form of *be used to* or *get used to* and the verb in brackets.

1 Julia kept drinking lots of water. She isn't _used to eating_ such spicy food. (eat)
2 I'm always losing my sunglasses. I haven't _____ them yet. (wear)
3 I'm finding it more difficult than I thought to _____ on the right. (drive)
4 My children are _____ because we travelled abroad when they were babies. (fly)
5 It's taken me ages, but I've finally _____ tea with milk. (drink)
6 Are you _____ in a country without seasons yet? (live)
7 My grandmother is now _____ emails, but she still can't use a mobile phone. (answer)

4 Will has just started working from home. Fill in the gaps with the correct form of these verbs.

| ~~waste~~ | enjoy | organise | focus | wear | have to | get |

1 Before I worked from home, I used to _waste_ at least three hours a day on the train.
2 I still can't get used to not _____ leave home at seven o'clock every morning.
3 I'm still not used to _____ my own working day. I get distracted easily.
4 I used to _____ chatting to people in the office so I sometimes feel a bit lonely.
5 I'm slowly getting used to _____ on work, rather than what's happening at home.
6 I'd find it difficult to get used to _____ suits and ties again instead of my jeans.
7 When I worked in an office, I never used to _____ home in time to go to the gym in the evenings.

5 Match sentence beginnings 1–6 to endings a–f.

1 There always   _f_
2 She can't get ___
3 She'll never   ___
4 Are you   ___
5 Did he   ___
6 He's never   ___

a getting used to your new school?
b used to getting up so early now she has this new job.
c got used to living in the country. He finds it strange.
d get used to the long winters in this country.
e use to be an actor at one time?
f used to be a lot of traffic on this road. What's happened?

6 Find one mistake in each sentence and correct it.

working
1 I'm not used to ~~work~~ so hard.
2 He's getting used to have a baby in the house.
3 He's use to driving long distances, so don't worry.
4 He used to the hot weather. He comes from Australia.
5 I didn't used to like him, but I do now.
6 We used to playing together when we were children.
7 Did you two used to know each other?
8 How long did it take to get used to wear contact lenses?

VOCABULARY 2C AND SKILLS: At a glance

Reading

1 Read the article about body language and match headings 1–4 to paragraphs A–D.

1 It's a small world ___
2 Don't jump to conclusions ___
3 First impressions ___
4 The rules of attraction ___

2 Read the article again and decide whether these sentences are true (T) or false (F).

1 [F] People don't usually form an opinion of someone before they've spoken to them.
2 [ ] People everywhere nod their head to say 'yes' and shake their head to say 'no'.
3 [ ] It is impossible to smile properly if you don't feel like it.
4 [ ] If we are attracted to someone, we often try to copy what they are doing.
5 [ ] The most universal form of communication is one we're not usually aware of.
6 [ ] Body language doesn't always mean what you think it does.

Word building (1): suffixes VOCABULARY 2.3

3 Complete the sentences with the correct form of the word in brackets. All the words are in bold in the article.

1 I try not to make _judgements_ about people just because of what they are wearing. (judge)
2 The new job I've been offered will give me a lot more _____ (responsible)
3 Do you have a _____ about where to have the meeting next week? (prefer)
4 I only have the _____ to do and then the report will be finished. (conclude)
5 A lot of these expressions _____ from other languages. (origin)
6 You should speak with more _____ if you want them to believe you! (convince)
7 That's a _____ unusual idea that you just came up with. (real)
8 What I just said to her wasn't intended as a _____ of her work. (criticise)
9 Unless you take off that hat, you won't be _____ at all. (recognition)

READING THE SIGNS

A Most experts agree that it only takes between 90 seconds and four minutes to decide what we think about someone. And in fact, 80% of the time, we reach a **conclusion** about someone based on body language, before that person has even opened their mouth! Of course, what you say later will matter, and this is your **responsibility**. However, you do need to get the body language right straight away or people won't stay around long enough to find out how fascinating you really are!

B Many gestures, such as how you say 'yes' or 'no', **originate** from a specific country, but others are universal. For example, all people wrinkle their noses and raise their top lip to show dislike or **criticism**. Everyone knows what a smile is, too, and when you're only pretending to smile. This is because muscles around the eyes are linked to the emotional part of your brain, so they only work when you really mean it. Also, to have any **conviction**, a smile will fade after a few seconds. Fake smiles tend to last much longer.

C There are also signals to tell us whether someone is attracted to us. When someone flirts with you, they will make eye contact. This **preference** is shown by enlarged pupils and they will blink more often. Admirers will also mirror your behaviour, often unconsciously. So if you lean forward or take a sip of a drink, you will find that they will do the same. However, there is another gesture we are probably unaware of, but which is used by every culture on Earth and which some experts claim is the most instantly **recognisable** non-verbal human greeting. When we first see someone we find attractive, our eyebrows rise and fall and if they feel the same, they raise their eyebrows, too. It's not surprising if you have never noticed this, since the whole process only lasts about a fifth of a second!

D However, don't make **judgements** about people on just one thing! Look for at least four signals. Sitting with their arms crossed might look as if someone is being defensive, but it might **really** mean they're feeling cold!

2D REAL WORLD — I see your point

Discussion language (1): agreeing and disagreeing politely REAL WORLD 2.1

1 Match phrase beginnings 1–8 to endings a–h.

1 Oh, do you — a still not convinced.
2 Oh, I b what you mean.
3 I can't c be right there.
4 I suppose — d think so?
5 Well, I'm e argue with that.
6 You might f a good point.
7 I see g wouldn't say that.
8 That's h that's true, actually.

2 Read opinions 1–6. Decide if **a** and **b** are agreeing (A) or disagreeing (D).

1 I think he's done really well as manager this season.
  a Oh, do you think so? _D_
  b I suppose you've got a point there. _A_

2 I think it's time people started supporting our local shops instead of using big supermarkets.
  a I wouldn't say that. ___
  b I can't really argue with that. ___

3 The government ought to fine people who don't recycle paper and plastic.
  a You might be right there. ___
  b I can't really see the point of doing that! ___

4 In my opinion, there's too much pressure on young people these days.
  a I see your point. ___
  b I don't know about that. ___

5 Footballers are paid far too much, if you ask me.
  a I suppose that's true, actually. ___
  b That's a good point. ___

6 The reason many people don't buy much organic food is because it's expensive.
  a Well, I'm still not convinced. ___
  b I see what you mean. ___

3 Read the conversations and fill in the gaps with these phrases.

> I can't really see the point of that.
> I see what you mean.
> Oh, do you think so?
> Well, I can't argue with that.
> Well, I'm still not convinced.

1 A My brother never lets his children watch TV at home.
  B _I can't really see the point of that._ They'll just watch it somewhere else instead.

2 A That film was really boring.
  B _____
  I quite enjoyed it.

3 A I don't eat red meat any more because all the evidence shows it's bad for you.
  B _____
  I'd prefer to see more research before I give it up.

4 A Experts are now saying that teenagers need at least ten hours' sleep a night.
  B _____
  Alex is always bad-tempered the next day if he stays up late.

5 A We think that making teenagers get a part-time job means they learn the value of money.
  B _____
  You're right, just as long as their school work doesn't suffer.

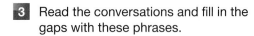

Reading and Writing Portfolio 2 p66

3A Against the law

Language Summary 3, Student's Book p132

Crime VOCABULARY 3.1
Criminals and crime verbs
VOCABULARY 3.2

1 Complete sentences 1–7 with the correct pair of crimes and crime verbs.

> ~~mugged/mugging~~   burglary/burgled
> theft/stolen   shoplift/shoplifting
> loot/looting   smuggle/smuggling
> vandalism/vandalise

1 I was _mugged_ recently. Some guy took my mobile. I reported the _mugging_ to the police.

2 If something is _____ from you, report the _____ to the police.

3 Graffiti is a common kind of _____ and costs the UK about £1 billion each year. Graffiti artists commonly _____ road signs and public transport.

4 High taxes in Britain in the 18th century led to a dramatic increase in _____. The most common items to _____ into Britain were tobacco and alcohol.

5 There are over 30 million instances of _____ in British stores each year. If you _____ in the UK and are caught, you will almost always be prosecuted.

6 There was a lot of _____ in New Orleans immediately after Hurricane Katrina. Even the police had to _____ fuel from abandoned cars in order to drive their police cars.

7 My parents were _____ last year. The criminals got in through an open window. It was my parents' first _____ and they were upset.

2 Complete the puzzle with words for criminals.

Someone who …

1 intentionally damages property belonging to other people. (6)
2 takes a person and holds them prisoner, often in order to demand money. (9)
3 takes things or people to or from a place illegally. (8)
4 obtains money by deceiving people. (9)
5 sets fire to things illegally. (8)
6 illegally enters buildings and steals things. (7)
7 attacks people, often in the street, to steal something. (6)
8 commits violent crimes, often for political reasons. (9)
9 steals things from shops and homes during a disaster, for example a riot or war. (6)

(Crossword: 1 down VANDAL)

Second conditional; alternatives for *if* GRAMMAR 3.1

3 Match sentence beginnings 1–8 to endings a–h.

1 If someone mugged you and took your keys,   _h_
2 It's very hard to prove a case of arson   ___
3 Even if I was offered a lot of money,   ___
4 As long as you could prove the credit card was stolen,   ___
5 Their parents would be furious   ___
6 If I saw someone shoplifting,   ___
7 Suppose you found out your brother was a burglar,   ___
8 If I found some money in the street, I might keep it,   ___

a I'd never take a bribe.
b you wouldn't be responsible for paying the bill.
c would you tell the police about him?
d if they knew their children had vandalised the phone box.
e assuming I didn't know who had lost it.
f unless the criminal is caught at the scene.
g I might try and tell someone.
h ~~would you change the locks in your house?~~

15

4 Choose the correct word and write the correct form of the verbs in brackets.

1. A *Supposing*/*Assuming* you _realised_ (realise) your young son had accidentally left a shop holding a £25 toy, would you take it back?
   B Yes, I might. *Imagine*/*As long as* it _____ (not be) too far away.

2. A *If*/*Provided* you _____ (break) something expensive in a shop and no one saw you, would you tell anyone?
   B Never. *Provided*/*Unless* I knew they _____ (not charge) me for it.

3. A _____ you _____ (approach) a group of teenagers *if*/*imagine* you saw them vandalising something near your house?
   B Definitely. *Even if*/*Assuming* they _____ (look) threatening. I can't stand vandalism.

4. A *Imagine*/*Assuming* you _____ (hit) a car in a car park and there were no witnesses. Would you leave a note?
   B Of course. *Assuming*/*Supposing* the other car _____ (be) damaged.

5. A *Even if*/*Suppose* you were hungry in the supermarket and you _____ (eat) something while you were walking round, would you pay for it at the checkout?
   B Yes. *Provided*/*Unless* I _____ (forget) about it, of course!

6. A *Suppose*/*As long as* you heard a good CD at your friend's house. _____ you _____ (ask) him to make a copy or buy it yourself?
   B I would usually buy my own copy. *Provided*/*Unless* I _____ (can) find it in the shops, of course.

3B It shouldn't be allowed!

Crime and punishment VOCABULARY 3.3

1 Read the article and choose the correct words.

CRIMES OF THE FAMOUS

Celebrities may lead unimaginable lifestyles but they still have to follow the law. And if they ¹ _commit_ a ² _____, they can be sure the whole world will be watching.

In court – Winona Ryder

American actor Winona Ryder shoplifted $5,000 of clothes and bags from a shop in New York. The shop ³ _____ her to court and the jury ⁴ _____ her guilty. The judge ⁵ _____ Winona to 480 hours of community service – helping the local community. He also ⁶ _____ her $10,000. Winona didn't work again for five years.

Coldplay's lead singer, Chris Martin, was more fortunate. He was ⁷ _____ for vandalising a photographer's car in Australia. The photographer was taking pictures of Chris while he was surfing.

However, Chris didn't even have to go to ⁸ _____ because a few months later the police dropped the charges.

The rapper Snoop Dogg's case was more serious: murder. After a three-month trial, Snoop was ⁹ _____ of the crime and released immediately.

Some celebrities have a longer criminal record. James Brown, the soul singer, was first ¹⁰ _____ to prison when he was 15 for stealing some clothes. During his life, he was arrested eight times!

	a	b	c	d
1	(a) commit	b give	c do	d convict
2	a court	b crime	c guilty	d prison
3	a sentenced	b sent	c arrested	d took
4	a sentenced	b found	c fined	d convicted
5	a gave	b sent	c sentenced	d charged
6	a gave	b committed	c took	d fined
7	a arrested	b acquitted	c committed	d found
8	a guilty	b evidence	c crime	d court
9	a convicted	b charged	c acquitted	d found
10	a found	b sent	c charged	d arrested

Third conditional GRAMMAR 3.2

2 Choose the correct verb forms.

1 If I *would have accepted/had accepted* your offer of a lift, I *would have/had* got home safely.
2 *Would you have/Had you* moved here if you *would have/had* known about the crime problem?
3 If he *had/'d had* a weapon, I *hadn't had/wouldn't have* tried to stop him.
4 Suppose they *had/had been* caught you, *did you have to/would you have had to* pay a fine?
5 He *would of/could have* committed the same crime again if the judge *hadn't sentenced/didn't sentence* him to prison.
6 Imagine you *didn't have/hadn't had* your mobile, what *had you/would you have* done?
7 If we *wouldn't have/hadn't known* about his criminal record, we *wouldn't had/might not have* suspected him.
8 How much would *have you/you have had* to pay, if they *would have/had* found you guilty?

3 a Complete the third conditional sentences with the correct form of these verbs.

> ~~not have/not arrest~~   not attack/shoot   take/not refund
> go/find   not give/acquit   get/not become

1 If we _hadn't had_ any evidence, we _wouldn't have arrested_ him.
2 _____ you _____ the company to court if they _____ your money?
3 Suppose he _____ her, _____ she _____ him?
4 She _____ to prison for a long time if they _____ her guilty.
5 He _____ away with it if we _____ suspicious.
6 If she _____ evidence, the jury _____ him of the murder.

b Read the sentences in **3a** again. Are these sentences true (T) or false (F)?

1 a [F] The police didn't have any evidence.
  b [ ] The police arrested him.
2 a [ ] The company gave the money back.
  b [ ] You took the company to court.
3 a [ ] He attacked her.
  b [ ] She shot him.
4 a [ ] She went to prison for a long time.
  b [ ] She was found guilty.
5 a [ ] He didn't get away with it.
  b [ ] We became suspicious.
6 a [ ] She gave evidence.
  b [ ] He was found guilty of murder.

4 Write sentence chains using the third conditional.

1 Rachel wasn't well → She took a day off work → She was in bed at midday → She heard her neighbour's alarm → She saw the burglars → She called the police

If Rachel had been well, she
wouldn't have taken a day off work.
If she hadn't taken a day off she
wouldn't have ...

2 Martin didn't have a job → Martin didn't have any money → He stole some food from a supermarket → The security guard called the police → Martin had to go to court → He went to prison → He met lots of criminals → He became interested in crime → He trained as a police officer.

If Martin had had a job,

VOCABULARY 3C AND SKILLS: The cost of crime

Reading

1 Read the first part of the article below. Which two subjects <u>doesn't</u> it mention?

a Some places where CCTV is installed.
b The cost of CCTV.
c The popularity of CCTV in the UK.
d The shop owner's reason for installing CCTV.
e What criminals think of CCTV.

Verbs and prepositions   VOCABULARY 3.4

2 Read part 1 again and choose the correct prepositions.

In my local corner shop a few weeks ago, I mentioned having an unwanted TV to the owner, Rizza. His normally bored face lit up. Within ten minutes we were back at my flat, apologising ¹*to/for/about* my wife ²*of/for/with* the noise – it was late – as we dragged an ancient TV out of the loft.

"It really is quite old," I said. But Rizza insisted ³*of/to/on* taking it, saying it was perfect for the shop. I assumed he meant for entertainment during quiet periods.

A few days later, I was in Rizza's shop again and I spotted our old TV. On the screen I saw a picture of myself.

"Security cameras," Rizza announced, "to catch shoplifters." I look around the shop. It's a tiny place. Only a magician could succeed ⁴*after/in/for* taking anything without being seen.

"Great!" I say.

Rizza's decision to install closed-circuit television (CCTV) is not unusual. The number of CCTV cameras throughout the UK has been estimated as high as four million. However, recent research, based ⁵*on/of/in* the number of cameras in an average town, thinks the number is closer to two million. You don't need to apply ⁶*with/to/of* anyone ⁷*to/from/for* permission to install a CCTV camera. So, they are everywhere: from busy shopping centres to the quietest corners of public parks.

---

3 Read the second part of the article below. Fill in the gaps with the correct verb and preposition.

| worry | cope | ~~convinced~~ | complained | stops |
| with | to | from | ~~of~~ | about |

Most British people support CCTV. It makes areas feel safer, they say. It discourages crime and helps to solve it, they add. And if you've ever seen CCTV images of a criminal on the news, it's hard to disagree. However, many others are not ¹ _convinced_ ² _of_ its effectiveness. There is no clear evidence that CCTV ³_____ criminals ⁴_____ committing crimes.

Opponents also ⁵_____ ⁶_____ the issue of personal privacy. A few years ago Geoffrey Peck felt unable to ⁷_____ ⁸_____ his life. He attempted suicide in a British street and he was spotted by a CCTV camera. The police were called and fortunately he survived. However, the pictures were shown on TV – to approximately nine million viewers – and Geoffrey's face was clearly visible. He ⁹_____ ¹⁰_____ the police about this and was awarded £7,000 compensation.

I passed my local shop again the next week. Rizza was repairing the glass door with his son. Neither of them looked very happy. "Thieves broke in last night," he explained.

"Oh, no!" I replied. "Have you watched the CCTV yet?"

"There are no CCTV pictures," he said unhappily, pointing to his son. "He turned the camera off when he left the shop last night!"

WARNING CCTV IN OPERATION

4 Read the complete article and answer these questions.

1 What did the writer think Rizza wanted the TV for?

2 What does the writer think of Rizza's idea? Why?

3 What reason does the writer give for the large number of CCTV cameras?

4 Why do some people like CCTV?

5 What arguments against CCTV does the writer mention?

6 Why did Geoffrey Peck get £7,000?

7 Did Rizza's CCTV help after the break-in at his shop? Why?/Why not?

REAL WORLD 3D — How can I help?

Making, refusing and accepting offers REAL WORLD 3.1

1 Complete the conversations with these phrases.

> ~~Let me help~~   you wouldn't mind   That'd be
> if you like   I'd better   Would you like me

FRAN ¹ _Let me help_ you tidy up.

EMMA Thanks. ² _____ a great help. It'll take me ages otherwise.

JIM I'll ring someone about the broken window, ³ _____ .

EMMA No, thanks. ⁴ _____ call the insurance company myself. They'll have a number for a repair person.

JIM OK. ⁵ _____ to check upstairs?

EMMA Are you sure ⁶ _____ ? I'm sure they've gone, but I haven't been up there yet.

> What if I called   I can   As long as
> would it help if   It'd be easier   Why don't I

PAM Who would vandalise your car? ⁷ _____ call the police?

BETH No, don't worry. ⁸ _____ if I called them when I get home. I'm meant to pick up Michael at three.

MARK It'll take me half an hour, but ⁹ _____ I changed the wheel?

BETH Oh yes. ¹⁰ _____ you don't mind. Thanks so much. I'm useless at that kind of thing.

PAM ¹¹ _____ the school and told them you'll be late? I'll explain why.

BETH No, that's OK. ¹² _____ call Michael on his mobile. He's old enough to get a taxi home.

2 a Make offers with these words.

1 you / out / Let / take / me / dinner / to .
   Let me take you out to dinner.

2 me / over / Would / come / like / you / to ?
   _____

3 your / bank / it / if I / rang / help / Would ?
   _____

4 cancelled / meeting / if / morning's / What / tomorrow / I ?
   _____

5 call / I / you / a / Why / taxi / don't ?
   _____

6 you / like / you / pick / you can / stay at ours / up and / I'll / tonight if .
   _____

b Match sentences 1–6 in **2a** to replies a–f.

a _1_ No, it's OK, but thanks for asking. I'm not really very hungry. I think I just need an early night.

b ___ Are you sure you wouldn't mind? They took my mobile.

c ___ No, thanks. I'd better do it myself. It won't take long to cancel my cards.

d ___ Well, it'd be wonderful if you could. I need some company and I don't want to stay here.

e ___ No, that's OK. I can ask my son to come round. He'll stay here tonight.

f ___ As long as you don't mind. We could rearrange it for next Monday.

> Reading and Writing Portfolio 3 p68

19

4A Urban legends

Language Summary 4, Student's Book p134

Phrasal verbs (1)

VOCABULARY 4.1

1 a Replace the words in bold with the correct form of a phrasal verb in the box.

| go off | ~~get away with~~ |
| make up | pass on |

1 My brother always **escapes punishment for** being late for work. _gets away with_

2 I couldn't think quickly enough, so I **invented** an excuse. _____

3 The smoke alarm **made a noise** when I burnt some toast. _____

4 Could you remember to **give** this message to your parents, please? _____

b Fill in the gaps with the correct form of a phrasal verb in the box.

| turn out | run away | work out |
| come round | ~~knock out~~ | |

1 I had a fight with my brother and he accidentally _knocked_ me _out_.

2 Luckily, after the accident I _____ _____ again quite quickly.

3 My brother was so frightened of what I might do that he _____ _____ .

4 The film began badly, but it _____ _____ to be worth staying for.

5 Can you give me a few moments to _____ _____ what I owe you?

Narrative verb forms; Past Perfect Continuous

GRAMMAR 4.1

2 a Read the first part of the story and choose the correct verb.

Andy ¹jogged/(was jogging) through the park one day on his way to the shops when another jogger ²bumped/was bumping into him. The other jogger ³apologised/was apologising to Andy and then ⁴was going on/went on running. Feeling a little annoyed, Andy then ⁵noticed/had noticed his wallet ⁶went/had gone. So he ⁷was chasing/chased the jogging pickpocket through the park. When he ⁸had caught up/had been catching up with him, he ⁹shouted/had shouted, "Give me that wallet!"

b Read the second part of the story. Choose one of the verbs a, b or c.

The frightened robber did what he ¹ _b_ and then ² _____ as quickly as he could. Anxious to tell someone about what ³ _____ , Andy went straight home, where his wife, Barbara, ⁴ _____ for him to return. As soon as he came in the door she asked him why he ⁵ _____ to the shops. Andy ⁶ _____ , saying that he ⁷ _____ a good excuse. Barbara ⁸ _____ , "I know you have. You left your wallet on the table."

	a		b		c
1	was saying		said		had been saying
2	ran away		was running away		had been running away
3	happened		was happening		had happened
4	was waiting		had waited		waited
5	didn't go		hadn't been going		hadn't been
6	was apologising		apologised		had apologised
7	had had		was having		had
8	replied		was replying		had been replying

3 Make sentences with these words, using the Past Simple, the Past Perfect Simple or the Past Perfect Continuous.

1 By the time Sam / get / home from school, / his friends / eat / all the cake.
 By the time Sam got home from school, his friends had eaten all the cake.

2 When I finally / find / the café, / Jacqui / already / wait / for an hour.
 _____

3 By the time I / get / out of the shower, / the phone / stop / ringing.
 _____

4 When we / arrive / at the cinema, / the film / already / start.
 _____

5 When Tom / come / to see me, I / feel / exhausted / because I / work / all day.
 _____

4 Read the story and fill in the gaps with the verbs in brackets. Use the Past Simple, Past Perfect Simple or the Past Perfect Continuous. Sometimes more than one answer is possible.

Late one evening Charlie ¹ _came out_ (come out) of a shop where he ² _____ (buy) some bread and milk. Suddenly he ³ _____ (realise) that his car ⁴ _____ (disappear). Nobody in the shop ⁵ _____ (notice) anything because they ⁶ _____ (do) their shopping.

However, the next day the owner of the shop ⁷ _____ (phone) Charlie to tell him to come back right away. When he ⁸ _____ (get) there he ⁹ _____ (see) his car in the same place that he ¹⁰ _____ (park) it the night before. On the window there was a note which said "Sorry, but my wife was having a baby and I ¹¹ _____ (have to) take her to hospital urgently."

Charlie was very relieved and told the police that his car ¹² _____ (be) returned. However, when he ¹³ _____ (get) home he discovered that someone ¹⁴ _____ (steal) his TV and computer. On the table was a note reading "Sorry, but I need the money for the kid's education."

4B First books

Books and reading VOCABULARY 4.2

1 Complete the puzzle. Find a kind of book. ↓

1 The page that lists the articles or parts in a magazine or book. (8, 4)
2 Another word for writer. (6)
3 The story of a book, film or play. (4)
4 Someone who writes books about imaginary people and events. (8)
5 Books with the same style or topic are in the same literary _____ . (5)
6 Walk around a shop looking at things, but not planning to buy them. (6)
7 A book that has a thick, stiff cover. (8)
8 Someone whose job it is to make judgements on books, films, etc. (6)
9 Look quickly through the pages of a book, newspaper or magazine. (5)

Defining, non-defining and reduced relative clauses GRAMMAR 4.2

2 a Read these descriptions of books and plays and add commas to the non-defining relative clauses.

1 This book which was about the American Civil War was made into a famous film.
2 This Shakespeare play is about two lovers whose families hate each other.
3 The place where this modern novel takes place is Paris.
4 This novel which is by the Russian writer Tolstoy is extremely long.
5 This book whose hero is a vampire is very popular with teenagers.
6 The novel that I love the best was written by a Frenchman called Flaubert.

b Do you know the films and books in **2a**? If you do, match the descriptions 1–6 to the titles a–f.

a ___ War and Peace
b ___ Romeo and Juliet
c ___ Twilight
d ___ Madame Bovary
e ___ Gone with the Wind
f ___ The Da Vinci Code

3 Read this interview with a person who has started a reading group. Cross out any words in bold which you can leave out.

CAREY What exactly is a reading group?
POLLY Well, it's basically a few people ¹**who** meet from time to time to talk about what they liked and disliked about books ²~~which~~ they've all read.
CAREY What made you decide to set one up?
POLLY I think the main reason ³**that** we started it was to provide a focus for people to meet and talk about something other than their work or family!
CAREY And what kind of people do you invite?
POLLY Oh, the people ⁴**who** come range from young mums to professional writers!
CAREY Who decides on the books ⁵**that** you're going to read?
POLLY We all do! Whoever comes to the meeting decides on one to read next time.
CAREY How often do you meet?
POLLY The number of meetings ⁶**that** we have will depend on how busy we all are. No more than one a month.
CAREY Do you ever invite guest speakers?
POLLY We do occasionally invite someone ⁷**whose** book we find particularly interesting, but only if they live fairly near.

4 Read this description of a novel and fill in the gaps with *who, that, which, whose, where* or *when*.

A book ¹ _that_ I really used to love when I was a child was *Black Beauty*. It's a story ² _____ takes place in 19th-century England at a time ³ _____ people were often cruel to animals. It's a kind of autobiography written from the horse's point of view about its experiences with a variety of owners.

As a young horse, Black Beauty lives happily in a place ⁴ _____ everyone is kind to him. Unfortunately, when the owner has to go abroad, he sells him to a family ⁵ _____ are not so kind. He goes on to have a lot of bad experiences, ⁶ _____ is the sad part of the story, but it does all end happily in the end.

Although people think of it as a children's book, this is a novel ⁷ _____ helped to influence thinking about the way we treat animals and so it's a book ⁸ _____ message is timeless.

5 Complete sentence b with the information in a.

1 a Can I borrow that Steve Jobs biography? Jill was reading it last night.
   b Can I borrow that Steve Jobs biography _(which/that) Jill was reading_ last night?

2 a The novel is based on a true story. Her mother told her the story.
   b The novel is based on a true story _____.

3 a My son lent me this book. I'm trying to finish it before he gets back.
   b My son lent me this book, _____ gets back.

4 a I know that woman. She's giving a reading from her book tonight.
   b I know the woman _____ tonight's book reading.

5 a Did you read that paperback? I lent it to you last week.
   b Did you read that paperback _____ last week?

6 a Jacqueline Wilson is a writer. Her books are read by millions of young girls all over the world.
   b Jacqueline Wilson is a writer _____ millions of young girls all over the world.

22

VOCABULARY 4C AND SKILLS Very funny!

Reading

1 Read the article quickly. What is it about?
a an unfortunate job interview
b a new television comedy
c an amusing human error

Connecting words: reason and contrast VOCABULARY 4.3

2 Choose the correct words 1–6 in the article.

3 Read the article again and choose the best answers to complete the sentences.

1 Guy Goma had gone to the BBC TV centre because
 a he wanted a job.
 b someone had phoned for a taxi.
 c he was being interviewed on TV.

2 The confusion happened because
 a Mr Goma didn't speak any English.
 b there were two men called Guy.
 c there were two IT experts at the BBC.

3 When Mr Goma realised he was on TV, he
 a panicked.
 b went completely quiet.
 c pretended nothing was wrong.

4 The BBC staff
 a realised their mistake immediately.
 b didn't realise their mistake at first.
 c didn't realise their mistake until the interview had finished.

5 Mr Goma
 a has become well known.
 b found the experience funny.
 c will be paid a lot of money by the BBC.

The wrong GUY!

THE STORY OF GUY GOMA IS NOT ONE OF STUPIDITY. A former taxi driver from the French Congo, Mr Goma was at the BBC TV centre for an interview, in the hope of becoming an IT assistant. So when a producer came up to him and said, "Guy Kewney, isn't it? About the IT thing?" he agreed, ¹*because/due to* he thought she had just pronounced his surname badly.

Mr Goma, who had taught himself English after he moved to England four years previously, was rushed into a studio, where he found himself in front of the cameras, having questions thrown at him. How could he know that the man who'd been sitting on a nearby sofa was also called Guy? In fact Guy Kewney was an IT expert, who was waiting to go on live TV to be interviewed about a legal dispute with Apple computers.

"It all happened so fast," Goma told *The Sun* newspaper. "I had just signed my name in reception when someone said 'Follow me'. She was walking so fast that I had to jog to keep up with her. ²*Even though/However* a lady put some make-up on me and I was fitted with a microphone, I just thought it was all part of the job interview and when I realised I was on air, what could I do? I just tried to answer the questions and stay calm."

Viewers of the most-watched TV interview in months – it was posted on YouTube – have reacted with a mixture of delight and sympathy to the key moment when the BBC's Karen Bowerman introduced Goma as "Guy Kewney, head of newswireless.net!" Across his expressive face flit a dozen expressions in a second – mainly shock, fear, guilt and embarrassment – as he wondered what to do next. However, ³*instead of/apart from* saying there had been a mistake, he answered three questions before the BBC staff became aware of what had happened and brought the item to an early close.

Mr Goma was finally taken to his interview for the IT post, but ⁴*even though/despite* going through such a bad experience, he didn't get the job. ⁵*Nevertheless,/Whereas* Mr Goma is now in demand as a celebrity, ⁶*due to/since* hundreds of thousands of people have now watched his television appearance online.

4 Complete this summary of the article with these connecting words.

| ~~because of~~ apart from even though whereas instead of as |

1 Guy Goma was at the BBC __because of__ a job interview.
2 _____ the two men had the same name, the producer got confused.
3 _____ the producer said the wrong name, Guy still went with her.
4 Guy Kewney is an IT expert, _____ Guy Goma is an IT assistant.
5 Mr Goma tried to answer the interviewer's questions _____ explaining it was a mistake.
6 _____ looking a bit shocked, Goma gave no other sign that there was something wrong.

23

4D REAL WORLD: How was your day?

Ways of exaggerating VOCABULARY 4.4

1 Complete these conversations. Make words with the letters in brackets.

1 A Shall I make you a sandwich?
   B I'd love one. I'm _starving_ . (vtangrsi)
2 A I think you need a break! I'll look after the kids.
   B Would you? They've been _____ me _____ all day. (vdrgini/rzayc)
3 A Are those shoes too small for you?
   B I think they must be. My feet are _____ me. (nklgili)
4 A What was the motorway like on the way back?
   B Very busy. It was a complete _____! (gmernitha)
5 A Will you be late home again?
   B I'm afraid so. This work is taking _____. (ofrveer)
6 A Can I get you some water?
   B Please. I'm _____ for a _____. (gydni/kridn)

2 Complete the conversations with these phrases.

| a fortune | scared stiff | speechless |
| out of my mind | over the moon | a ton |

1 A Did you buy that dress in the end?
   B No. It was lovely but it cost _a fortune_ .
2 A Could you give me a hand moving this cupboard?
   B Sorry, I've tried but it weighs _____!
3 A Clare seems very happy today!
   B Yes, she's _____ about passing her driving test.
4 A Surely you're not frightened of spiders?
   B I'm absolutely _____!
5 A Did you have a good evening?
   B No, I didn't. Mike was late back and I was going _____ with worry.
6 A Were you surprised by the lovely things they said about you?
   B Surprised? I was completely _____!

Saying you're surprised or not surprised
REAL WORLD 4.1

3 a Make phrases with these words.

1 not / Oh / again / no _Oh no, not again_ !
2 imagine / I / can _____.
3 wouldn't / he / say / He / would / that _____?
4 is / news / fantastic / That _____!
5 honest / be / to _____
6 bet / you / I / were _____!

b Fill in the gaps in the conversation with phrases 1–6 in 3a.

LAURA Sorry I'm late. My car broke down again this morning.
BECKY ᵃ _Oh no, not again!_ That's the third time this week.
LAURA I know. Anyway, it took the mechanic two hours to arrive, so I was a bit annoyed, to say the least.
BECKY ᵇ _____ So would I have been! Did he have an excuse?
LAURA Not really. He just said it wasn't his fault.
BECKY ᶜ _____ Did he manage to fix it?
LAURA He did. But I'm sick of the car now, ᵈ _____ I'm going to get a new one. How are you, anyway?
BECKY Great, actually. I've just heard I've got a place at university.
LAURA Wow! ᵉ _____ Well done.
BECKY It's such a relief.
LAURA ᶠ _____ Let's go and celebrate!

Reading and Writing Portfolio 4 p70

5A Nature's best

Language Summary 5, Student's Book p137

Adjectives (1) VOCABULARY 5.1

1 Replace the phrases in bold with these adjectives.

| weird | enthusiastic | rewarding | rare |
| lucrative | ~~time-consuming~~ | fierce | |

time-consuming

1 Keeping a pet can be **something that takes up a lot of time** but it can also be **something that gives you a lot of satisfaction** if you do it well.
2 Rats can seem **very strange or unnatural** pets but the British first started keeping them over 150 years ago.
3 Pet smuggling can be **something that makes a lot of money** for criminals.
4 Monkeys are fortunately **uncommon** as pets because they need constant attention and can be **physically violent** towards people.
5 Children are usually **interested in and excited** about pets for the first few months but many will lose interest in their animals after this.

2 Make a word from box A and box B to describe these pets.

A
~~exot~~	faith
unsuit	destruct
harm	affection

B
able	less
~~ic~~	ate
ful	ive

1 *exotic* : There are an estimated 15,000 lions, tigers and other big cats kept in private homes in the US.
2 _____ : I don't think a snake is a good pet for a five year-old.
3 _____ : Mark's cat loves sitting on people.
4 _____ : Thomas has a snake but it's a non-poisonous one.
5 _____ : Chihuahuas love chewing sofas and cushions.
6 _____ : Sally's dog is always with her, like a best friend.

Ways of comparing GRAMMAR 5.1

3 a Match sentences 1–5 to replies a–e.

1 I think spiders are far scarier pets than snakes.   *e*
2 Keeping a rabbit is no harder than keeping a goldfish. ___
3 Hippos are not nearly as friendly as I thought they would be. ___
4 Cats are nowhere near as hard work as dogs. ___
5 A ticket to our local zoo is nearly as expensive as going to a concert! ___

a Yes, they're a great deal easier to look after, aren't they?
b Yes. And it's only slightly cheaper for children than adults.
c I agree. It's just as easy.
d That's right. They're considerably more dangerous than people think.
e ~~Yes, they frighten me almost as much as rats.~~

b Underline the comparative phrases in **3a** and fill in the gaps in the table.

1 I think spiders are <u>far scarier pets than</u> snakes.
e Yes, they frighten me <u>almost as much as</u> rats.

no difference	1 _____ , 2 _____
a small difference	3 *almost as much as* , 4 _____ , 5 _____
a big difference	6 *far scarier than* , 7 _____ , 8 _____ , 9 _____ , 10 _____

4 Read the introduction to an article. Choose the correct words.

Over a million people in the UK keep some kind of exotic pet. Although that's considerably ¹(*fewer*)/*less* people than those who have a cat, it's ²*near*/*nearly* as many as the number of people who own a goldfish.

Why would anyone decide to keep a snake as a pet? They're only slightly more attractive ³*as*/*than* tortoises. They're nowhere near as ⁴*cute*/*cuter* as rabbits. And they're ⁵*far*/*more* harder to look after than many other pets.

Last week I met Carla, who has had pet snakes for almost ten years. Keeping snakes as pets, she told me, is ⁶*much*/*lot* less unusual than I might expect. I must admit I was considerably ⁷*fewer*/*less* enthusiastic than Carla about meeting her two pythons, Bart and Lisa. Unlike their cartoon 'cousins', Bart is not ⁸*anywhere*/*quite* as lively as Lisa and sits quietly throughout our conversation. Lisa, on the other hand, is clearly ready to play.

"Don't worry," says Carla. "She's ⁹*no*/*not* more dangerous than me."

Read the rest of this article here.

25

5 Complete sentence b so it has the same meaning as a. You can use between three and five words, including the word in brackets.

1   a   Cats are much easier to look after than dogs.
    b   Cats are _nowhere near as difficult_ to look after as dogs. (nowhere)
2   a   Goldfish are a lot cheaper than koi.
    b   Goldfish are _____ koi. (nearly)
3   a   Tortoises are far less interesting than snakes.
    b   Tortoises aren't anywhere _____ snakes. (near)
4   a   Butterflies have considerably larger wings than bees.
    b   Butterflies' wings _____ than bees' wings. (deal)
5   a   Tortoises aren't quite as easy to look after as goldfish.
    b   Goldfish are _____ look after than tortoises. (little)
6   a   Many people think dolphins are no more intelligent than whales.
    b   Many people think whales are just _____ dolphins. (as)

6 Correct the mistakes.

                                    half as
1   An adult shark is ~~as half~~ big as an adult whale.
2   Rabbit's fur is as softer as feathers.
3   There are thousands more leopards in the world that tigers.
4   Bee stings are a lot painful than mosquito bites.
5   The number of wild tigers is getting smaller and smaller than each year.
6   Spiders are farther more frightening than ants.

5B Royal treasures

Phrasal verbs (2) VOCABULARY 5.2

1 Complete the sentences with the phrasal verbs.

| ~~cheer up~~   go ahead   packed out   fit in with |
| put out   pass by   catch up on   talk into |

1
DEBBIE Come out with us tonight. It'll _cheer_ you _up_ .
CLARE No, I'm fine. I want to _____ some work. I'm really behind at the moment.

2
RUTH Martin says he wants to come on holiday but he's happy to _____ our plans.
PAUL OK. I'll _____ and book the flights then.

3
MAX I often _____ your house on the way home. Are you busy on Wednesday?
PAT It'd be lovely to see you but I don't want to _____ you _____ .

4
SIMON I can't believe I let Sally _____ me _____ going to Windsor on Friday.
ALEX You're mad! It'll be _____ with families at this time of year.

Future verb forms; Future Continuous GRAMMAR 5.2

2 Correct the mistake in each sentence.

                    to
1   We're going ^ visit Buckingham Palace.
2   If you need me, I'll have be sitting outside in the garden.
3   They're comeing to lay a new lawn this afternoon.
4   I'm going to buying some fresh herbs.
5   The castle doesn't opens until ten.
6   The pollen probably will make me sneeze.
7   I'll watering the plants if you like.
8   I imagine we'll been working in the garden all weekend.

3 Match sentences 1–8 in **2** to meanings a–h. Then fill in gaps A–E with these verb forms.

| ~~be going to~~ | Future Continuous | will |
| Present Simple | Present Continuous | |

A *be going to*

  a *1* for making predictions based on present evidence.

  b ___ for personal plans or intentions.

B _____

  c ___ for fixed events on a timetable.

C _____

  d ___ for future arrangements.

D _____

  e ___ for actions that will be in progress at a point in the future.

  f ___ for something that will happen in the normal course of events.

E _____

  g ___ for instant decisions.

  h ___ for predictions not based on evidence.

4 Choose the correct future form.

1 It says here that the pottery class *will be beginning/(begins)* at 6.30.

2 Look at all those trees. You're *having/going to have* to clear up a lot of leaves in the autumn.

3 You'll *be seeing/seen* her soon, won't you?

4 I'll *give/'m giving* her a rabbit for her birthday. It's at my house.

5 We're *finding/'ll find* the weather a lot warmer in the future.

6 *Are you going to/Do you* get a pet of any kind?

7 I've got an idea! I'll *use/'m using* that tree trunk to make logs for the fire.

8 We *watch/'ll be watching* you in the race on television.

9 I'm *waiting/'ll be waiting* outside your house tomorrow morning at six o'clock.

10 They'll *have/be having* enough time if they leave right now.

5 Complete the conversations with the correct future forms of the verbs in brackets.

1 PRESENT CONTINUOUS; WILL

JESS What's that book? Don't tell me you ¹ *'re thinking* (think) of getting an iguana!

RAY Yes. I ² _____ (probably get) one. But I'm not completely sure.

JESS ³_____ (you be able) to look after it?

RAY I ⁴_____ (go) on a course about keeping exotic pets next week. So we ⁵_____ (see).

2 FUTURE CONTINUOUS; PRESENT SIMPLE

MAX I ⁶_____ (not come) in tomorrow morning.

LENA Why not?

MAX Well, if my train to London ⁷_____ (go) at one, I won't have time.

LENA Yes, you will. I ⁸_____ (leave) work at around midday for a meeting in town, so I can take you to the station.

MAX OK. But we must leave on time. Traffic ⁹_____ (get) terrible around the station during the lunchtime rush hour. And if I ¹⁰_____ (miss) my train, I ¹¹_____ (ask) you for a lift to London!

6 Complete the sentences with the Future Continuous form of these verbs.

| ~~have~~ wonder stay meet think fly |

1 When they arrive we *'ll be having* dinner.

2 I _____ of you while you're in your exam.

3 I _____ her again in a few weeks if you want to come.

4 I should go. My mum _____ soon where I am.

5 At midnight we _____ somewhere over the Atlantic.

6 _____ you _____ at home this evening?

27

VOCABULARY 5C AND SKILLS: The nature of cities

Reading

1 Read the first two paragraphs. What is unusual about the River Ebro in Zaragoza?

A Nobody knows how the huge catfish got in the river.
B There are bird-eating fish that live in the river.
C Pigeons lie in wait to attack the giant fish living in the river.

2 Read the whole article and decide whether the following sentences are true (T), false (F) or the article doesn't say (DS).

1. [T] The threat to pigeons started quite recently.
2. [ ] The catfish only ever attacks pigeons.
3. [ ] The townspeople had first told the writer about the strange attacks.
4. [ ] The best time for people to go and watch the unusual sight is later in the day.
5. [ ] The best time to see the attacks is while there is still daylight.
6. [ ] People living in the town tend to sympathise with the pigeons.

Guessing meaning from context

VOCABULARY 5.3

3 a Look at the six words in bold in the article and put them in these groups.

verbs	1 _loiter_
	2 _____
nouns	3 _____
	4 _____
adjectives	5 _____
	6 _____

b Match the words in **3a** to the meanings a–f. Look carefully at the context.

a do something slowly, or wait for no reason _____
b attack suddenly _____
c careless _____
d enormous _____
e bird _____
f wait quietly and secretly _____

Pigeon fanciers

In the Spanish city of Zaragoza, a new menace is threatening the city's pigeons and it comes from the depths of the River Ebro. Every day, birds living in the historic buildings there fly down to drink at the base of a nearby bridge. Some never return.

The reason for their disappearance is the **giant** wels catfish, a species native to central and eastern Europe that grows up to three metres long. The catfish were introduced to the Ebro by German fishermen in the late 1970s but in the past couple of months the catfish have begun to **lurk** in the waters around the bridge. When pigeons **loiter** too long at the water's edge, a fish leaps up from below and swallows one of them whole.

The citizens of Zaragoza, fascinated, gather at the bridge each day to witness the unlikely battle between fish and **fowl**. Having heard about this unusual event in the Spanish media and thinking it was worth investigating, I decided to join them.

I arrived at the bridge on a chilly afternoon. There were no catfish in sight, however. No pigeons, no crowds, nothing. But as the day went on, more and more passers-by paused to take a quick glance into the depths. I talked to one, named Oscar, who helpfully showed me the stretch of water where the catfish liked to be.

Not everyone was so well informed. One self-appointed expert confidently told me that catfish weren't fish at all, because they live on both land and in water. Another know-it-all explained that they only fed in the morning. (I found out later that they actually hunt in the evening and at night.)

Finally, at about 5.30 in the afternoon, a dark shape measuring a good deal more than a metre took up its place in the water close to the **unwary** birds, which were drinking nearby. By now, an audience had gathered in the hope of a show – and it didn't take long. With a sudden splash, a catfish made an unsuccessful **lunge** at a pigeon. The next bird was not so lucky. For two hours, a crowd of about 50 watched three big catfish feeding.

Most people were taking the side of the fishy invaders. A cheer went up whenever a catfish made a successful attack. One woman was on the pigeons' side, however, greeting each narrow escape with a shout of triumph. "Poor things," she said. "Nobody likes them."

5D REAL WORLD: Carbon footprints

Adjectives for giving opinions VOCABULARY 5.4

1 Replace the words/phrases in bold with these adjectives.

| illegal | justifiable | ethical | wasteful | damaging |
| unsustainable | disturbing | inevitable | | |

illegal

1 Building here without permission is **not allowed by the law**.
2 I believe that a world shortage of oil is **certain to happen** if we continue to be so **inefficient and careless**.
3 The current rate of oil consumption is **impossible to maintain**.
4 The environmental impact of tourism can be **shocking and upsetting**. But many governments think it is **acceptable** because of the business it generates for their economies.
5 Can producing cigarettes ever be **morally correct** when they are so **harmful** to our health?

Discussion language (2): opinions REAL WORLD 5.1

2 Match sentences 1–6 to replies a–f.

1 It'd be much better if everyone were charged for the amount of rubbish they produced. *b*
2 One argument in favour of organic food is that it simply tastes better. ___
3 How many languages will die out before the end of the century? ___
4 So you're saying that the Earth will be uninhabitable by 2100? ___
5 What proportion of the world's population doesn't have access to clean water? ___
6 I just don't think it's right that over half of the world's population live in poverty. ___

a Maybe, but I don't see how we can change the situation.
b I've never really thought about that. But it does sound a good idea.
c It's hard to say. But estimates say about half of the existing number.
d Yes, but then again it often costs twice as much.
e Er, let me think. About 1 billion people so that's about 15%.
f No. That's not what I meant. All I'm saying is that it's going to get a lot warmer.

3 Fill in the gaps in the conversations with these phrases.

It'd be much better if	Maybe, but I just don't
No, that's not what I	That's an interesting
I don't think it's right	Yes, but then again
One argument in favour of	
Well, some people would	
I've never really thought about	

A

PIA ¹ *It'd be much better if* everyone bought fruit locally.
TOM ² _____ argue that it would be a bit boring. Imagine if we didn't have bananas.
PIA ³ _____ , imagine how interesting it would be when you travelled abroad.

B

BEN ⁴ _____ nuclear power is that it's relatively cheap.
JOAN ⁵ _____ that. But doesn't it produce a lot of waste?
BEN ⁶ _____ point. In fact, very little waste, but the waste is highly dangerous.

C

ALAN ⁷ _____ that we waste so many resources on transport.
LILY ⁸ _____ see how we can stop people from buying cars.
ALAN ⁹ _____ meant. All I'm saying is that our oil supplies are not sustainable.

Reading and Writing Portfolio 5 p72

6A Codes of conduct
Language Summary 6, Student's Book p140

Phrases with *take*
VOCABULARY 6.1

1 Match sentences 1–10 to endings a–j.

1 Don't take any notice _i_
2 I sometimes feel my family take me too much ___
3 It was really kind of him to take the time ___
4 My son has never taken an interest ___
5 My daughter always takes it out on me ___
6 OK, do you mind taking responsibility ___
7 I've learned never to take sides ___
8 Does your brother still take life ___
9 This time, I won't take no ___
10 Don't let your boss take advantage ___

a when she's in a bad mood.
b too seriously? If so, he needs to let go a bit!
c in any kind of sport.
d to explain the rules to us.
e for granted. I wish they'd help more.
f of you. You are supposed to finish at six.
g for organising the picnic?
h when the two of them have arguments.
i of Joe if he shouts at you. He does it to everyone.
j for an answer. You have to let me pay.

Uses of verb+*ing* **GRAMMAR 6.1**

2 Fill in the gaps with verb+*ing*. Use the verbs in the box.

| ~~live~~ chat annoy waste go try enjoy apologise be |

After ¹ _living_ in France for a few months, I realised that I really should stop ² _____ to be so polite all the time. The French seem to find it ³ _____ if you say things like "I'm awfully sorry" because they feel you are ⁴ _____ their time. It must seem to them that the British spend their whole time ⁵ _____ ! The French don't really make 'small talk' either. ⁶ _____ to strangers such as taxi drivers or shop assistants, especially politely, is seen as rather strange. Another difference is that people ⁷ _____ to dinner parties in France will expect to take part in a serious discussion, with guests often ⁸ _____ asked their opinions on 'big issues'. British people, despite ⁹ _____ discussions about house prices and education, are sometimes surprised if their guests want to talk about anything serious, such as politics or art.

3 Make sentences with these words.

1 fascinating / culture / has / Japan / a .
   Japan has a fascinating culture.
2 humour / don't / living / understand / here / British / Despite / I .
   _____
3 People / you / close / some / standing / like / cultures / too / don't / in .
   _____
4 countries / expensive / in / Eating / some / is / restaurants / in .
   _____
5 direct / try / to / questions / avoid / I / answering .
   _____
6 much / being / how / English / earn / The / they / asked / hate .
   _____

4 Complete sentence b so it means the same as sentence a, using verb+ing.

1 a If you queue-jump you can make some people very angry.
  b _Queue-jumping_ makes some people very angry.
2 a People are no longer allowed to smoke in many public places.
  b _____ is now forbidden in many public places.
3 a People talk about the weather as a way of starting a conversation.
  b _____ is how many people start a conversation.
4 a It is rude to be very late for appointments or meetings.
  b _____ for appointments or meetings is rude.
5 a When business people meet for the first time, they usually shake hands.
  b _____ is normal when business people meet for the first time.
6 a People who speak loudly in public on mobile phones are often seen as rude.
  b _____ in public on mobile phones is often seen as rude.
7 a Much of the population enjoys watching soap operas.
  b _____ is very popular with much of the population.
8 a Many people find it embarrassing to complain in restaurants.
  b _____ in restaurants is embarrassing for many people.

5 Are the words/phrases in bold correct? Change the incorrect phrases.

1 This morning I was woken early by the neighbour's dog **bark** loudly.
2 **Feel** a bit annoyed, I decided to get up.
3 Before **going** downstairs I had a shower and got dressed.
4 Suddenly, **I was noticing** that my front door was open.
5 I could see a red car **being driven** away at top speed.
6 Someone had broken into my house and escaped, **take** my new TV with them.

6B ▸ Rebel!

Compound adjectives describing character

VOCABULARY 6.2

1 Read the conversations about three people who have applied for a job. Look at the phrases in bold. Choose three adjectives from the box to describe each person.

> ~~self-assured~~   big-headed   self-conscious
> laid-back   absent-minded   level-headed
> narrow-minded   self-centred   strong-willed

A

ANNA Joanne's certainly very ¹**confident**! She's only been here a few weeks, but you wouldn't believe it!
ANDY Mmm, confident, certainly. Some might say ²**she thinks she's more important than she really is.**
ANNA True, and ³**she has a very clear idea of exactly what she wants to achieve**, which is good as long as she's prepared to listen to other people too.

Joanne is ¹ _self-assured_ , ² _____ and ³ _____ .

B

ANDY And what about Steve?
ANNA Well, ⁴**he's calm and sensible when he's making decisions.**
ANDY Is he? Interesting. But am I right in thinking that ⁵**he's more interested in himself than in other people?**
ANNA Yes, that's fair enough. And ⁶**he's not as open to new ideas as he could be**, which would be a bit of a problem, working with so many new people.

Steve is ⁴ _____ , ⁵ _____ and ⁶ _____ .

C

ANDY I really like Emma, myself. ⁷**She's a very relaxed kind of person.**
ANNA That's true. Except giving presentations in front of a lot of people – then ⁸**she does get a bit embarrassed.**
ANDY Yes, I'd noticed that. And ⁹**she tends to forget things, too.** She doesn't always concentrate that well.
ANNA So who is it to be, then? Joanne, Steve or Emma?

Emma is ⁷ _____ , ⁸ _____ and ⁹ _____ .

Modal verbs (1); levels of certainty about the future GRAMMAR 6.2

2 Are sentences 1–8 correct? Change the incorrect sentences.

               'll get
1 I shouldn't think she ~~gets~~ the job.
2 They are bound preferring Emma.
3 I don't suppose they will come.
4 I doubt if Steve won't apply for the job.
5 She's unlikely having another interview.
6 They may well want to talk to us.
7 I can't imagine they choose her for the job.
8 They are sure to come late.

3 Complete the conversations with the words/phrases in the boxes.

A

| will | bound to | doubt | may well | unlikely |

ERIN Do you think Jess ¹ _will_ get the job?
LIZ Oh, she's ² _____ . Everyone thinks she's wonderful!
ERIN But she ³ _____ decide not to apply for it.
LIZ I ⁴ _____ that, myself. She's quite ambitious.
ERIN Yes, you're right. She's ⁵ _____ to be happy earning this salary for very long!

B

| couldn't | dare say | can't imagine |

AL I ⁶ _____ they'll stop paying overtime, surely?
OLIVE They might. I ⁷ _____ there's a lot of pressure on them to save money at the moment.
AL I know. Even so, they ⁸ _____ do that without lots of people being very angry.
OLIVE Well, we'll soon find out!

4 Complete these sentences about the future, using the words in brackets.

1 Take your coat. It's _bound to rain_ if you don't. Look at those clouds! (bound/rain)
2 Don't worry if you forget her birthday.
  I _____ (not/suppose/she/mind)
3 I don't think we should wait for him.
  I _____ this late. (doubt/he/arrive)
4 We don't need to pack many clothes.
  I _____ at this time of year. (can't imagine/it/be/cold)
5 Give him a ring. He's _____ about it if we don't. (likely/forget)

5 a Write sentences with these words.

1 Matt / bound / ask Charlotte out soon.
  Matt is bound to ask Charlotte out soon.
2 I / not imagine / what / happen / in the next episode of *High Street*.

3 I / not suppose / Bruce / get back / from lunch before two.

4 It's unlikely / Ellie / invite us to her party now.

5 I dare say / Jamie / be / play / computer games again, as usual.

b Match sentences 1–5 in **5a** with replies a–e.

a ___ You never know, she might, but we're not too popular at the moment.
b ___ He may well be. He certainly seems to be busy with something.
c ___ Actually, I know. I'll tell you, if you want.
d ___ I doubt it. He usually takes at least an hour, especially if he's meeting Laura.
e ___ He may, but I don't think for one second she'll say yes.

VOCABULARY 6C AND SKILLS > Dress code

Reading

1 Read the article about dress codes in UK schools. Is the answer to the question in the title *yes* or *no*, according to the headmaster?

Back referencing VOCABULARY 6.3

2 Read the article and look at the words in bold. What do they refer to, a or b?

	a		b	
1	a	the school	b	its students
2	a	the dress code	b	the exam results
3	a	at the school	b	in the countryside
4	a	uniforms	b	beliefs
5	a	from Europe	b	from the UK government
6	a	schools	b	uniforms
7	a	wearing appropriate clothes	b	what students wear
8	a	the pupils'	b	the school's

3 Are the sentences true (T), false (F) or the article doesn't say (DS)?

1. [F] Anthony Gell school is known for doing exceptionally well academically.
2. [ ] Headteachers in the UK are not allowed to go against government policy on uniforms.
3. [ ] Pupils at schools with a uniform policy do not necessarily all achieve the minimum educational requirements.
4. [ ] David Baker abolished uniform at his school when he became headmaster.
5. [ ] Students at Anthony Gell sometimes choose to wear clothes which identify them with that school.
6. [ ] At Anthony Gell, richer children do not make fun of those with less expensive clothes.
7. [ ] David Baker rates clothing as less of a priority than helping pupils to learn.
8. [ ] There are no guidelines about what to wear at Anthony Gell.

Are uniforms the key to educational success?

THERE'S an unusual school hidden away in the English countryside. Anthony Gell is a small comprehensive, ¹**which** successfully supports its students and involves the local community. It also achieves good exam results, but ²**that's** not what makes it stand out. What makes it distinctive is that there is no dress code ³**there**.

In Europe, school uniforms are relatively rare. Yet the UK government has had a firm belief in the power of uniforms for years now, linking ⁴**them** to high standards and strict discipline and advocating zero-tolerance of untidy dress.

Headteachers have found it hard to resist ⁵**such** pressure. Over 90% of secondary schools are now thought to insist on uniforms and most of the ⁶**others** enforce a strict dress code. However, despite dressing students in blazers and ties, more than 40 schools still failed to reach the government's target for basic subjects, and an eight-year research project in the US recently concluded that uniforms do not make schools perform better.

When he became head of Anthony Gell, a non-uniform school, David Baker was aware of how this issue divided people – even the students themselves. But after doing an extensive survey, he decided not to change. "As long as students come in appropriate clothes, ⁷**this** isn't an issue. I believe in treating children as individuals, with rights and responsibilities."

Supporters of uniforms insist they improve behaviour and community spirit. Yet recent inspections of Anthony Gell commented on how responsible the pupils appeared and on their obvious pride in and loyalty towards the school.

Interestingly, proof of Anthony Gell's good relations with its pupils is revealed by ⁸**their** willingness to buy its optional branded clothing. Students are frequently seen wearing hoodies and sweatshirts adorned with the school logo around town at the weekend.

Another claim made for uniforms is that they paper over divides between rich and poor children, making bullying less likely. But Baker maintains that this is not a problem specific to schools and that wearing a uniform doesn't solve it. The dress code at his school is simple: "3Cs – clean, comfortable and covered up." And the absence of a school uniform liberates him from the obligation to enforce it, thus allowing more time to focus on the important business of teaching and learning.

6D Sorry to interrupt ...

Polite interruptions REAL WORLD 6.1

1 Find one mistake in each sentence and correct it.

1 Is this good time?
   Is this a good time?

2 Sorry to disturbing you.
   _____

3 Can I have word?
   _____

4 Sorry bother you, but have you got a minute?
   _____

5 I was wondering if could I see you for a moment.
   _____

2 Complete the conversations using the sentences in 1 and the words in brackets.

1
LUCY Hi, love. ¹ *Is this a good time?*
BEN Hi. It isn't, I'm afraid. (against / really / the / up / I'm / moment / at / it) ² _____
LUCY That's OK, I'll catch you later.
BEN See you!

2
DAN Hi, Paul. ³ _____
PAUL Sorry, mate, you can't. (tied / just / I'm / bit / up / now / a) ⁴ _____
DAN Don't worry. It can wait.
PAUL Cheers.

3
JUAN Hello. ⁵ _____
SARA I haven't just now, I'm afraid. (time / Sorry, / a / this / good / isn't) ⁶ _____
JUAN Don't worry. Some other time?
SARA Yes, of course. Shall we try later on today? Around 5?

4
SUE Hello. ⁷ _____
CLARE That's fine. But (pushed / at / I'm / the / for / time / moment / rather) ⁸ _____
SUE It's not important. I'll come back later.
CLARE Great. See you then.

5
SIMON Excuse me, ⁹ _____
KAY I wish I had the time, Simon. But (busy / really / I'm / rather) ¹⁰ _____
SIMON When would be more convenient?
KAY Let me just have a look in my diary.

Review: future verb forms

3 Read the conversation and choose the correct verb forms.

NINA Hi, James, sorry to disturb you at work.
JAMES It's no problem. Are you OK?
NINA I'm fine. I was just thinking about this evening. Do you know what time the film ¹*starts*/will start?
JAMES I'm fairly sure it's 7.30.
NINA I thought so. ²*Are you going to/Do you* meet us for a drink first or not?
JAMES Probably not. I think ³*I'll be working/I work* late again, so ⁴*I'll probably meet/I'm probably meeting* you there as usual.
NINA Right. Amanda ⁵*is coming/will come*, too, by the way. I invited her this morning.
JAMES Good. ⁶*I'm going to/I'll* give you both a lift home, if you like.
NINA That's brilliant, because the last train ⁷*will go/goes* at ten and that means we ⁸*won't have to/aren't having to* rush to catch it.
JAMES OK. See you later.
NINA Bye.

Reading and Writing Portfolio 6 p74

7A At the airport

Language Summary 7, Student's Book p142

State verbs VOCABULARY 7.1

1 Read the quotations. Fill in the gaps with the state verbs in the boxes.

| ~~seem~~ realises trusts doubt deserves |

Can I quote you on that?

1 " Very few of us are what we _seem_ . "
   Agatha Christie, writer (1890–1976)

2 " The old believe everything, the middle-aged _____ everything, the young think they know everything. "
   Oscar Wilde, writer (1854–1900)

Agatha Christie

3 " By the time a man _____ that maybe his father was right, he usually has a son who thinks he's wrong. "
   Charles Wadsworth, priest (1814–1882)

4 " He who allows himself to be insulted, _____ to be. "
   Pierre Corneille, writer (1606–1684)

5 " No one believes the official spokesman, but everyone _____ an unidentified source. "
   Ron Nessen, politician (1934–)

| suit respect involve recognise |

6 " Experience is that marvellous thing that enables you to _____ a mistake when you make it again. "
   Franklin P. Jones, journalist (1908–1980)

7 " Sometimes I wonder if men and women really _____ each other. Perhaps they should live next door and just visit now and then. "
   Katharine Hepburn, actress (1907–2003)

Katharine Hepburn

8 " Tell me and I'll forget; show me and I may remember; _____ me and I'll understand. "
   Chinese proverb

9 " When you are content to be yourself and not compare or compete, everybody will _____ you. "
   Lao Tzu, philosopher (551–479 BC)

Simple and continuous aspects; activity and state verbs GRAMMAR 7.1

2 a Match sentence beginnings 1–6 to endings a–f.

1 Many of the workers here _e_
2 Yesterday morning the queues at check-in ___
3 At least three times a year ___
4 The airline provided ___
5 During his university holidays, Mark ___
6 My family and I have ___

a I fly back to our head office in the US.
b been waiting in this queue for over three hours.
c is working for an airline.
d were making everyone very bad-tempered.
e ~~live within ten kilometres of the airport.~~
f food and drink for passengers during the delays.

b Circle the correct answers.

Which sentences from **2a** describe:

a something unfinished? 2 or ⑥
b something permanent? 1 or 5
c something temporary? 3 or 5
d a habit? 1 or 3
e something completed? 4 or 6
f something in progress at a specific time? 2 or 3

3 Read about Wayne's job. Choose the correct verb form.

I work for an airline as a Customer Service Agent. That means I ¹(look)/am looking after passengers from the moment they arrive at the check-in desk until they board the plane. I ²do/'ve been doing this job since I left school, but the stress ³starts/is starting to get me down. This morning I ⁴do/'m doing check-in. Generally, I ⁵have to/'m having to check people's tickets and passports. It can be a nightmare! Last week, I dealt with a businesswoman who ⁶flew/was flying to Dubai to give a speech at a conference. She ⁷had brought/had been bringing her daughter's passport instead of hers! By the time her passport ⁸arrived/was arriving – in a taxi – her flight had left. I ⁹think/'m thinking about applying to be a flight attendant. I ¹⁰'ve talked/was talking to a few the other day and they ¹¹seemed/were seeming so positive about what they do every day. I ¹²suspect/'m suspecting you need a lot of patience to do their job, though!

4 Fill in the gaps with the correct form of the verbs in brackets.

1 I _'m seeing_ the doctor tomorrow. I _have_ an appointment at ten. (see, have)
2 _____ you _____ the queues at the airport on the news last night? I _____ of cancelling my flight. (see, think)
3 Toby _____ very strangely today. _____ you _____ we should call the vet? (behave, think)
4 I _____ this mobile for over three years so I _____ of changing it. (have, think)
5 I didn't even say 'hello' when I _____ him yesterday. I _____ a bad day. (see, have)

7B Showpiece of China

Business and trade VOCABULARY 7.2

1 Change the word at the end of each line to complete the encyclopaedia entry.

www.freepedia.com/capitalism

Capitalism

CAPITALISM is an economic system in which money is ¹ _invested_ in the ² _____ of goods and services which are then sold for profit. Since the 17th century, capitalist ³_____ have been common in Western Europe. After the ⁴_____ Revolution, capitalism spread outside Europe to many other economies all over the world.

There are many criticisms of the system. ⁵_____ make much more money than the workers who actually ⁶_____ the items. The system leads to an unfair ⁷_____ of wealth – with the ⁸_____ of large gaps between the rich and the poor. Furthermore, it needs constant economic growth and, therefore, ⁹_____ claim that capitalism will one day be responsible for using the last of the world's natural resources.

Many ¹⁰_____, however, point out that capitalist countries have a higher than average income and life expectancy.

INVEST
PRODUCT
ECONOMY
INDUSTRY

MANUFACTURE
PRODUCT
DISTRIBUTE
DEVELOP
ENVIRONMENT

ECONOMY

Present Perfect Simple and Present Perfect Continuous GRAMMAR 7.2

2 Choose the correct ending for sentences 1–8.

1	They've been trying …	a	to sell their house before, but no one was interested.
2	They've tried …	b	to sell their house for over a year now.
3	He's been asking me …	c	for help several times today.
4	He's asked me …	d	to help him all morning.
5	I've visited …	e	many industrial cities, but nothing compares to this one.
6	I've been visiting …	f	my relatives all weekend.
7	I've run …	g	and I'm absolutely exhausted.
8	I've been running …	h	over 30 kilometres this week.

3 Look at the pictures. Write sentences with the Present Perfect Continuous form of these verbs.

| ~~clean~~ snow decorate drive rise fall |

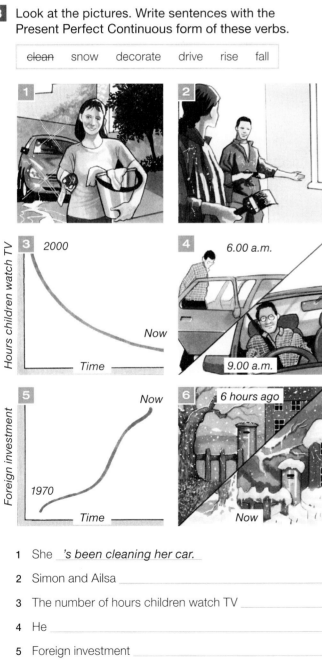

1 She *'s been cleaning her car.*
2 Simon and Ailsa _____
3 The number of hours children watch TV _____
4 He _____
5 Foreign investment _____
6 It _____

4 Fill in the gaps with the Present Perfect Simple or the Present Perfect Continuous of these verbs. Use the same verb in each pair of sentences.

| ~~go out~~ learn try reply phone paint |

1 a Have you *been going out* with each other for long?

  b He's not here. He's *gone out* with a friend for the evening.

2 a How many times _____ he _____ today?

  b I _____ you all morning.

3 a We _____ Spanish for three years and we still can't speak it very well.

  b _____ you ever _____ a foreign language?

4 a What's that on your jeans? _____ you _____ ?

  b I _____ my bedroom wall three times, but I can still see the old colour underneath.

5 a I _____ to over ten emails already today.

  b I _____ to emails all day.

6 a That car _____ to overtake us for the last few miles.

  b This is the most interesting food I _____ in a long time.

VOCABULARY 7C AND SKILLS — Life online

Word building (2): prefixes — VOCABULARY 7.4

1 Rewrite the sentences with a prefix and the word in bold.

| ~~pre~~ | non- | under | post- | pro- | ex- | mis |

1 We were invited to **view** the exhibition before it opened.
   We were invited to a _preview_ of the exhibition.

2 People often **pronounce** my name wrongly.
   People often _____ my name.

3 He used to be a **colleague**.
   He's an _____ .

4 Do any TV stations in your country support the **government**?
   Are any TV stations in your country _____ ?

5 She isn't **qualified** enough for the job.
   She is _____ for the job.

6 My new flatmate isn't a **smoker**.
   My flatmate is a _____ .

7 Our house was built after the **war**.
   Our house was built _____ .

Reading

2 Read the article about blogging. Fill in the gaps with the correct prefix.

| multi- | ~~re~~ | over | anti- | self- |

3 Are the sentences true (T), false (F) or the article doesn't say (DS)?

1 [DS] Visitors to Justin Hall's website were mainly people from his college.
2 [ ] Justin invented the word 'blog'.
3 [ ] *Blogger.com* was the first website that helped people publish their blog.
4 [ ] Blogging became a lot more popular after blogger.com.
5 [ ] Ellen lost her job over some comments on her company's blog.
6 [ ] The most popular blogs are written by famous people.
7 [ ] Some bloggers are paid through advertisements on their blogs.

Popular Culture › Blogging

One of the first blogs is thought to be Justin Hall's *Links from the Underground*. At this time, the web was a great deal smaller and Justin was a 20-year-old college student. People visited Justin's blog to find links to new and interesting websites. At the same time, they read Justin's honest and detailed account of his life. His blog continued for over ten years.

Three years after Justin's first post, someone came up with a term for what he, and other people, were writing – a weblog. The word comes from the words *web* and *log**. Then in 1999 another online diarist ¹ _re_ **wrote** the word as 'we blog' and soon the English language had a new word.

> **blog**: *noun* /blɒg/ [C] (also **weblog**)
> **Definition**
> a diary (= regular record of your thoughts, opinions and experiences) that you put on the Internet for other people to read.

The early bloggers needed some technical computing skills to make their pages. But from 1999, websites such as blogger.com started appearing. They made it simple for anyone to ²_____**publish** online and the phenomenon of blogging exploded. By 2001, there were about a million blogs on the Internet – from personal family blogs, with just a few readers, to blogs about news events read by thousands daily.

Several blogs have become news themselves over the years. Flight attendant Ellen Simonetti was fired by her airline for talking about her job on her blog. Some people have even gone to prison for ³_____**government** comments on their blog.

There are now over 150 million public blogs. This is probably an ⁴_____ **estimate**, as some of these are never updated. They are written by the young and old, the famous and unknown. Schools have them, companies have them, and there is one for every subject you can imagine.

Blogs that are very popular can earn their writers a living, too. Advertising on blogs is now a ⁵_____ **million** dollar business for companies like Google. Every time someone clicks on an advertisement on a blog, the blogger (and Google, of course!) get some money. The top 10 blogs each earn more than $1 million a year!

*log = a written record or diary

7D REAL WORLD ▶ You're breaking up

On the phone VOCABULARY 7.5

1 Complete the crossword.

1 an electronic answering system on your mobile where people can leave messages (9)
2 an agreement you sign with a mobile phone company before you get a phone (8)
3 a type of electronic display that can recognise when you put your finger on it (11)
4 If you don't have a 2, your mobile is this. (3-2-3-2)
5 If you lose 6 during a phone call, you get _____ . (3, 3)
6 The quality of the signal from your mobile network. (9)
7 a type of phone that is also a computer (10)
8 a phone connection that comes into your home (8)
9 the sound that your mobile makes when someone is calling you (8)

Problems on the phone REAL WORLD 7.1

2 Choose the best sentence for each situation.

1 Your friend tells you their mobile phone battery is getting low. Your friend says:
  (a) I think my battery's about to run out.
  b Shall I call you back on a landline?
  c You'll have to speak up a bit.

2 You're speaking to a friend, but you can't hear them clearly. You say:
  a There's a bit of a delay on the line.
  b I keep losing you.
  c Would you like me to phone you back?

3 Your friend's phone rings and you like the sound it makes. You say:
  a What's that ringtone?
  b Have you checked your voicemail?
  c Do you have a contract for your mobile?

4 While you're on your mobile, your train goes through a tunnel. You hear nothing your friend says. You say:
  a Sorry, it's a bad signal.
  b Sorry, you'll have to speak up a bit.
  c Sorry, I didn't catch any of that.

5 You're talking to a friend, but your phone is about to run out of money. You say:
  a Sorry, I'm just about to run out of credit.
  b Sorry, it's a bad line.
  c Do you want me to give you a ring later?

3 Complete the conversations with the phrases in the boxes.

| ~~about to run out of~~ | catch any of that |
| keep losing | breaking up | signal isn't very good |

ROB Hi, Dad. I can't speak for long. I'm ¹ *about to run out of* credit.
DAD Sorry, you're ² _____ a bit. I didn't ³ _____ .
ROB The ⁴ _____ here. I said my credit is low.
DAD I ⁵ _____ you, I'm afraid. I'll ring you back.

| calling you | my battery | got cut off | phone you back |

EVE Sorry, we ⁶ _____ .
NICK No, ⁷ _____ ran out, I'm afraid. I'm ⁸ _____ from a friend's phone.
EVE Ah, I see. Do you want me to ⁹ _____ ?

| my battery's about to | you'll have to speak up |
| on your landline | a bit of a delay |

DAN Wow! You're the other side of the world, but the line's perfect.
BEN Well, there's ¹⁰ _____ . And you're a bit quiet.
DAN Shall I call you back ¹¹ _____ ?
BEN No, don't worry. But ¹² _____ a bit.
DAN OK. Is that better?
BEN Yes. But unfortunately, ¹³ _____ run out!

Reading and Writing Portfolio 7 p76

Crossword across answers visible: 5C, 7 (across row with A, I, L shown vertically spelling VOICEMAIL down column 1)

8A I'm broke

Language Summary 8, Student's Book p145

Dealing with money VOCABULARY 8.1

1 Choose the correct words.

In the money?

Going through university is a huge financial challenge, with students increasingly getting part-time jobs to get them through their years of study. We asked four students at Birmingham University what they would do if they won a lot of money.

Jane, a first-year economics student, said, "I'd put most of my winnings into a ¹*current/savings* account so I could get a high interest ²*rate/rating*. Then I'd save up to go on holiday. I'd love to visit Australia." Her friend Claudia, who studies chemistry, was keen to ³*invest/repay* the ⁴*loan/credit* on her car before she did anything else so that she could stop worrying about how she would pay for it. Then, she added, "I'd spend the rest ⁵*for/on* my family for once because I'm always borrowing from them when I'm short ⁶*from/of* money."

Law student Rob told us, "It would be lovely to pay ⁷*money/cash* for something instead of always buying ⁸*in/on* credit." And Jason, in his final year of a computer science degree, said "If I were well ⁹*off/in*, the first thing I'd do is to invest money ¹⁰*on/in* an online business."

Wishes (1): *I hope ...; It's time ...* GRAMMAR 8.1

2 Look at the pictures and choose the correct sentences. Sometimes more than one answer is correct.

1 a I wish you came.
  b I wish you would come.
  c I wish you could come.

2 a If only I was well off.
  b If only I would be well off.
  c If only I were well off.

3 a I hope she arrives soon.
  b I hope she'll arrive soon.
  c I hope she arrived soon.

4 a If only I didn't have to get up.
  b If only I don't have to get up.
  c If only I wouldn't have to get up.

5 a It's time you go.
  b It's time to go.
  c It's time you would go.

6 a I wish he stopped.
  b I wish he stop.
  c I wish he'd stop.

3 Find six mistakes in this email and correct them. Sometimes more than one answer is correct.

Hi Jo,

I've been at college a month now, but it feels like I've been here all my life!

Hard work, but I'm enjoying it. I just wish I ~~have~~ *had* more money. I always seem to be overdrawn. At the moment I'm broke, but luckily it's nearly time for my parents sending me my monthly cheque. If only they send one every week!

Anyway, how are you? How's the new job? I wish you be here instead. It would be much more fun! If only there was a direct train service, you could come down more often. Anyway, it's about time I do some work. I haven't done any for two days. I hope you'd email me soon.

Suz x

4 Fill in the gaps in the conversation with the correct form of the verbs.

TOM I'm really fed up with this town. The transport situation is getting worse and worse.
BILL Yes, if only there ¹ _were/was_ (be) a decent bus service.
TOM You really need to have a car to live here, don't you? But I can't even afford a second-hand one at the moment.
BILL It's time we both ² _____ (find) jobs that paid better. I always seem to be in debt these days.
TOM Me too. I'm hoping someone at work ³ _____ (leave) soon, then I can apply for a promotion.
BILL I'm sick of living at my parents' house, that's my main problem. I'd love a place of my own.
TOM So would I. It's about time we ⁴ _____ (have) more independence, now we're 26!
BILL My mother's OK, I suppose. But she will insist on treating me like a child.
TOM That's mothers for you! Oh, well! Shall we go? I wish I ⁵ _____ (buy) you another drink, but I'm broke!

8B Every little helps

Phrasal verbs (3): money VOCABULARY 8.2

1 Complete the conversation with the prepositions.

| ~~into~~ out off (x3) back to down (x2) up |

SAM Apparently, Jane's aunt has died and she's come ¹ _into_ some money.
BOB Really? What's she going to do with it?
SAM Well, she's been saving ² _____ to go to Australia so maybe she'll do that, but first she wants to pay ³ _____ the mortgage on her flat.
BOB Oh, good. Maybe she can pay ⁴ _____ what she owes me, too!
SAM Or maybe she'll buy another property. Did you hear that house prices are set to go ⁵ _____ at last?
BOB Great. I've been waiting for that to happen before I took ⁶ _____ a mortgage myself.
SAM You do realise you have to put ⁷ _____ a much bigger deposit on a house than you used to, don't you?
BOB Oh, I'll borrow that from my parents.
SAM By the way, did you go to that new restaurant you were talking about?
BOB Yes, I did. I think they tried to rip me ⁸ _____ , actually.
SAM You're joking! What happened?
BOB Well, the bill came ⁹ _____ far more than we'd expected and it turned out they'd charged us for two bottles of wine instead of one. Having said that, they did take the extra money ¹⁰ _____ the bill when we complained. And they gave us a free drink too, which wasn't bad!

Wishes (2): should have GRAMMAR 8.2

2 Choose the correct verb forms.

DANI Oh no, look at all this traffic. We should ¹knew/_have known_ the motorway would be busy at this time of day!
RICK Well it's too late now! What time's the flight?
DANI In two hours. I wish I ²'d set/set my alarm an hour earlier.
RICK We should ³booked/have booked an earlier flight really! The traffic's always bad at this time.
DANI The early one was fully booked. Oh, dear. I wish we ⁴'d gone/went to the airport by train instead.
RICK But you said we had too much luggage, remember?
DANI I know, but we're going to miss the flight if the traffic stays like this.
RICK Well, frankly I wish we ⁵didn't decide/hadn't decided to go abroad at all. Airports are always a pain in August!
DANI Well, you should ⁶have told/told me earlier. You can organise it yourself next time!

3 Complete the article about past regrets with the correct form of the verbs in the boxes.

Things I regret

Wendy Miller, actress

~~have~~   give up
not listen   know   wait

I was an only child and I always wished I ¹ _'d had_ a sister or brother to play with. My parents bought me a puppy instead, but it wasn't the same! Then soon after I left drama school I married my husband. I wish I ² _____ a bit longer – he was a ski instructor, 20 years older than me, and I should ³ _____ it wasn't going to work out. Actually, I should never ⁴ _____ singing and dancing, either. I used to love appearing in musicals at drama school, but my tutor encouraged me to do more serious acting instead, so I joined the Royal Shakespeare Company. I do enjoy it, but thinking back, I wish I ⁵ _____ to her and just followed my own instinct. But we all make mistakes!

Bill Flack, businessman

work   spend   become
take   learn

Looking back, I definitely wish I ⁶ _____ harder at science at school, because, although I like my job, I should really ⁷ _____ a vet. Animals are my passion. I also wish I ⁸ _____ to play the saxophone at school. I'd love to have been in a jazz band. I should also ⁹ _____ a year off before university to travel abroad, because I think that's a really valuable experience that I missed out on. But more than anything, I wish I ¹⁰ _____ more time with my children when they were young, because they grow up so fast.

4 a Match the beginnings of sentences 1–6 to endings a–f.
1 I wish I'd   _c_
2 I wish I   ___
3 It's time you   ___
4 Don't you wish you   ___
5 They shouldn't   ___
6 Shouldn't he   ___

a did something about finding a job.
b have offered to pay back the deposit he borrowed from Amanda?
c known you were broke.
d had paid off your loan straight away?
e didn't have to work.
f have taken out such a huge mortgage.

b Match these sentences to 1–6 in **4a**.
a ___ They can't afford to pay it.
b ___ You've been living off your parents long enough.
c ___ I'd have lent you some money.
d ___ I'm sure she would like it back.
e ___ You must be paying so much interest on it.
f ___ I'd love to retire early.

5 Write sentences about the pictures.

1 I wish I / learn / to dance
_____

2 You shouldn't / park / here
_____

3 I wish I / not buy / so much
_____

4 I should / look / at the weather forecast
_____

VOCABULARY 8C AND SKILLS — A bit extra

Reading

1 Read the article quickly. According to the article, what do most employees prefer?

a flexible working hours
b a company car
c a free holiday

2 Which paragraph in the article:

1 says that different kinds of people should be offered different kinds of perks? C
2 suggests how smaller companies can afford to reward employees? ___
3 mentions the current popularity of relaxation therapies at work? ___
4 says how one company provides an exotic holiday as a work benefit? ___
5 gives examples of the ways employees can take a break from work? ___
6 talks about the growing importance of a shorter working day? ___
7 lists the most common ways of rewarding employees? ___
8 suggests that people value material perks less these days? ___
9 says which factors are most important to keep people in a job? ___

Synonyms VOCABULARY 8.3

3 Look at the words/phrases in bold in the article. Match them to their underlined synonyms in the article.

1 benefits – perks
2 _____
3 _____
4 _____
5 _____
6 _____
7 _____
8 _____

It's not just the MON£Y

A Not long ago, British entrepreneur Richard Branson announced that he had bought an island off the coast of Australia for all his 50,000 staff and their families to use. For employees of his company, Virgin, this must be one of the most attractive, if rather unusual, ¹**benefits** of the job!

B Most company perks are more practical than this, but they do appear to be an increasingly important consideration when choosing a job. Typical of these perks, but still valued, are ²**reductions** on the price of lunch, discounts on company goods or services, child-care facilities, interest-free loans and pensions and investments in the company. Particularly popular with employees is membership of a gym or health club and private health care. Keen to reduce sickness and stress, employers have generally been happy to support this trend and the past ten years have seen an increasing demand for on-site services such as massage and yoga. However, the appeal of perks such as cars, laptops or mobiles, which used to be a measure of a person's importance in the company, is declining in favour of benefits which better reflect the priorities of modern life. Material possessions are not the most important consideration these days.

C Surveys show that ³**pay** isn't ⁴**the be-all and end-all** once a person is settled in a job. Job satisfaction and personal achievement were named as the top motivators by almost 77% of managers recently, and recognition of their contribution was thought to be twice as important as a financial reward. Christine Garner, who is head of organisational development at the Industrial Society, believes that giving staff a choice of benefits showed that a firm was 'forward thinking'. "Parents may want to take ⁵**extra** holidays to be with their children. Older people may want more medical benefits and younger staff may prefer additional money."

D Richard Prior, spokesperson for the publishing house Redwood, thinks it's the little things that count and which are most ⁶**appreciated** by staff. Last year he announced that all staff could take the day off on their birthday, as well as leave early on Fridays in the summer. "We haven't got huge amounts of money to invest in perks, but little gestures can make a big difference." These may also include the chance to work at home sometimes, extra leave after a child is born, and US-style 'duvet days', when ⁷**employees** might decide to have a day's holiday without prior notice. Other companies let workers trade in some of their salary for extra ⁸**leave** or give them the opportunity to take time off to study or travel with the guarantee of a job when they return.

E Recent research has found that twice as many UK professionals would rather work fewer hours than win the lottery. Being able to choose when they work and what benefits are most appropriate allows employees to balance work and home life. It's fast becoming the number one perk.

8D REAL WORLD — I didn't realise

Apologising REAL WORLD 8.1

1 Put the conversation in the correct order. Sasha gives an apology and a reason, and Jill responds.

a No, she hadn't, but it doesn't matter.
b And I'm also sorry for not inviting Andrea to dinner last week.
c Forget about it. I borrowed Jim's.
d I had no idea you'd need the car.
e ~~I'm really sorry that I didn't get back home sooner.~~
f I thought Pam had done it, for some reason.

SASHA ¹ _e_ , ² ___
JILL ³ ___
SASHA ⁴ ___ , ⁵ ___
JILL ⁶ ___

2 Fill in gaps 1–4 with the phrases in box A. Then fill in gaps a–d with the phrases in box B.

A

| ~~I lost that pen you lent me~~   what I said yesterday |
| I'm so late   returning your call |

B

| to upset you   have put it down   for some reason |
| you'd phoned until a few minutes ago |

1
PAULA I'm sorry. I'm afraid ¹ _I lost that pen you lent me._
GILLIE Oh, that's alright.
PAULA I shouldn't ᵃ _____

2
ANDY I'm sorry for not ² _____
SIMON It doesn't matter.
ANDY I had no idea ᵇ _____

3
LUCY I'm sorry that ³ _____
BECKY Don't worry about it.
LUCY I thought you lived nearer, ᶜ _____

4
JOSH I'm sorry about ⁴ _____
NICK There's no need to apologise.
JOSH I didn't mean ᵈ _____

Review: relative clauses

3 Rewrite the information in 1–6 as one sentence, using relative clauses. Make any other changes you need.

1 Jodi Picoult is an American author. She has written more than 18 books since 1992.

   Jodi Picoult is an American author who has written more than 18 books since 1992.

2 She grew up in Long Island. It's an hour away from New York.

   _____
   _____

3 She is a best-selling writer. Her books are read all over the world.

   _____
   _____

4 Her books have been described as 'soap operas'. They deal with topics such as teenage issues and family problems.

   _____
   _____

5 She gets a lot of ideas for her books from her friends. They tell her all the gossip in the small town they live in.

   _____
   _____

6 She spends more than 100 days a year giving readings. She believes this helps to sell her books.

   _____
   _____

Reading and Writing Portfolio 8 p78

Answer Key

1A A global language

1 2 know a few words   3 can't speak a word   4 'm reasonably good   5 can also get by   6 picked up   7 'm bilingual   8 also fluent in   9 can have a conversation   10 it's a bit rusty

2 2 can get by in German   3 sister is fluent in Chinese   4 Portuguese is a bit rusty   5 picked up some/a few words of Italian on holiday   6 bilingual in Turkish and Spanish

3a 2 h   3 d   4 f   5 e   6 c   7 a   8 i   9 g
 b Present Continuous: 7   Present Simple passive: 8   Present Perfect Simple: 6   Present Perfect Continuous: 4   Past Simple: 1   Past Continuous: 3   Past Simple passive: 2   Past Perfect Simple: 5

4a 2 are based   3 was   4 had been   5 recovering   6 had just written   7 inspired   8 didn't   9 was   10 takes   11 believed   12 were
 b 2 was interrupted   3 were looking   4 gave   5 has had   6 still use / are still using   7 know   8 have recently asked   9 is written

1B Open learning

1 2 lecture   3 dissertation   4 fees   5 student loan   6 tutorial   7 Masters   8 undergraduate   9 postgraduate   10 professor

2a 2 Did you **go** to the seminar yesterday?   3 ✓   4 Some universities **do** give scholarships, but we don't.   5 ✓   6 If I were you, I **wouldn't** eat in the college canteen.   7 **Do** you like doing exams or prefer continuous assessment?   8 I've **been** invited to apply for a PhD, but the fees are too high.
 b b 1   c 7   d 6   e 8   f 5   g 3   h 2

3 2 a   3 a   4 c   5 b   6 a   7 c   8 c   9 b   10 a   11 b   12 c

4 2 wasn't   3 had   4 does   5 would   6 shouldn't   7 don't   8 'm   9 do   10 was   11 don't   12 won't

1C Getting results

1 c

2 2 to think   3 to recognise   4 to make   5 to check   6 making   7 think   8 reading   9 to suggest   10 to take   11 to demonstrate   12 be

3 1 B, E   2 D   3 G   4 F   5 A   6 C   7 B

1D Evening classes

1a 2 a   3 b   4 c
 b b 2   c 1   d 3

2 2 What about   3 Who to   4 Where from   5 How long for

3 2 was   3 How   4 Where   5 how's it   6 do you   7 What kind/type/sort   8 haven't you   9 like   10 what way

2A It's bad for you!

1a 2 every day   3 once in a while   4 every now and again   5 most days
 b 2 N   3 N   4 Y   5 Y   6 N   7 Y

2 2 happened   3 was always eating / always used to eat   4 he won't eat   5 he's always worrying   6 used to eat / would eat   7 he gets up   8 would even complain / was even complaining

3 3 ✓   4 used to be   5 knew / used to know   6 ✓   7 ✓   8 was / used to be   9 made

4 2 a   3 b   4 a   5 a

5 2 My doctor is always telling me to take more exercise.   3 My wife will (always) check the labels before she buys food.   4 When I was a student, I used to be a vegetarian.   5 I never used to worry about my food until I put on weight.   6 When my children were small, I would never give them fast food.

2B Life's different here

1 1 a   2 i   3 g   4 j   5 c   6 e   7 b   8 f   9 h   10 d

2 1 by   2 of   3 about   4 of   5 by

3 2 got used to wearing   3 get used to driving   4 used to flying   5 got used to drinking   6 used to living   7 used to answering

4 2 having to   3 organising   4 enjoy   5 focusing   6 wearing   7 get

5 2 b   3 d   4 a   5 e   6 c

6 2 He's getting used to **having** a baby in the house.   3 He's **used** to driving long distances, so don't worry.   4 He's used to the hot weather. He comes from Australia.   5 I didn't **use** to like him, but I do now.   6 We used to **play** together when we were children.   7 Did you two **use** to know each other?   8 How long did it take to get used to **wearing** contact lenses?

2C At a glance

1 1 B   2 D   3 A   4 C

2 2 F   3 T   4 T   5 T   6 T

3 2 responsibility   3 preference   4 conclusion   5 originate   6 conviction   7 really   8 criticism   9 recognisable

2D I see your point

1 2 g   3 e   4 h   5 a   6 c   7 b   8 f

2 2a D   b A   3a A   b D   4a A   b D   5a A   b A   6a D   b A

3 2 Oh, do you think so?   3 Well, I'm still not convinced.   4 Well, I can't argue with that.   5 I see what you mean.

3A Against the law

1 2 stolen; theft   3 vandalism; vandalise   4 smuggling; smuggle   5 shoplifting; shoplift   6 looting; loot   7 burgled; burglary

2 2 kidnapper   3 smuggler   4 fraudster   5 arsonist   6 burglar   7 mugger   8 terrorist   9 looter

3 2 f   3 a   4 b   5 d   6 g   7 c   8 e

4 1 As long as; wasn't   2 If; broke; Unless; wouldn't charge   3 Would; approach; if; Even if; looked   4 Imagine; hit; Assuming; was   5 Suppose; ate; Unless; forgot   6 Suppose; Would; ask; Provided; could

3B It shouldn't be allowed!

1 2 b   3 d   4 b   5 c   6 d   7 a   8 d   9 c   10 b

2 1 had accepted / would have   2 Would you have; had   3 'd had; wouldn't have   4 had; would you have   5 could have; hadn't sentenced   6 should be; would you have had to   7 hadn't known; might not have   8 you have had; had found

3a 2 Would you have taken; hadn't refunded   3 hadn't attacked; would she have shot   4 would have gone; had found   5 would have got; hadn't become   6 hadn't given; would have acquitted
 b 1b T   2a T   b F   3a T   b T   4a F   b F   5a T   b T   6a T   b T

4 1 ... been in bed at midday. If she hadn't been in bed at midday, she wouldn't have heard her neighbour's alarm. If she hadn't heard her neighbour's alarm, she wouldn't have seen the burglars. If she hadn't

Answer Key

seen the burglars, she wouldn't have called the police.
2 ... he would have had some money. If he'd had some money, he wouldn't have stolen food from a supermarket. If he hadn't stolen food from a supermarket, the security guard wouldn't have called the police. If the security guard hadn't called the police, Martin wouldn't have gone to court. If he hadn't gone to court, he wouldn't have gone to prison. If he hadn't gone to prison, he wouldn't have met lots of criminals. If he hadn't met lots of criminals, he wouldn't have become interested in crime. If he hadn't become interested in crime, he wouldn't have trained as a police officer.

3C The cost of crime

1 not mentioned: b, e
2 1 to 2 for 3 on 4 in 5 on 6 to 7 for
3 3 stops 4 from 5 worry 6 about 7 cope 8 with 9 complained 10 to
4 1 entertainment / watching TV 2 He thinks Rizza doesn't need CCTV because the shop is too small. 3 You don't need permission to install a CCTV camera. 4 It makes areas feel safer. / It discourages crime and helps to solve it. 5 There is no evidence that it stops criminals from committing crimes; there are problems with personal privacy. 6 Images of his suicide attempt were shown on TV. 7 No. The camera was turned off.

3D How can I help?

1 2 That'd be 3 if you like 4 I'd better 5 Would you like me 6 you wouldn't mind 7 Why don't I 8 It'd be easier 9 would it help if 10 As long as 11 What if I called 12 I can
2a 2 Would you like me to come over? 3 Would it help if I rang your bank? 4 What if I cancelled tomorrow morning's meeting? 5 Why don't I call you a taxi? 6 I'll pick you up and you can stay at ours tonight if you like.
b b 5 c 3 d 6 e 2 f 4

4A Urban legends

1a 2 made up 3 went off 4 pass on
 b 2 came round 3 ran away 4 turned out 5 work out
2a 2 bumped 3 apologised 4 went on 5 noticed 6 had gone 7 chased 8 had caught up 9 shouted
 b 2 a 3 c 4 a 5 c 6 b 7 c 8 a
3 2 When I finally found the café, Jacqui had already been waiting for an hour. 3 By the time I got out of the shower, the phone had stopped ringing. 4 When we arrived at the cinema, the film had already started. 5 When Tom came to see me, I felt exhausted because I had been working all day.
4 2 had bought/had been buying 3 realised 4 had disappeared 5 had noticed 6 had been doing 7 phoned 8 got 9 saw 10 had parked 11 had to 12 had been returned 13 got 14 had stolen

4B First books

1 2 author 3 plot 4 novelist 5 genre 6 browse 7 hardback 8 critic 9 flick ↓ paperback
2a 1 This book, which was about the American Civil War, was made into a famous film. 2 This Shakespeare play is about two lovers whose families hate each other. 3 The place where this modern novel takes place is Paris. 4 This novel, which is by the Russian writer Tolstoy, is extremely long. 5 This book, whose hero is a vampire, is very popular with teenagers. 6 The novel that I love the best was written by a Frenchman called Flaubert.
 b a 4 b 2 c 5 d 6 e 1 f 3
3 1 ✓ 2 which 3 that 4 ✓ 5 that 6 that 7 ✓
4 2 which/that 3 when 4 where 5 who/that 6 which 7 which/that 8 whose
5 2 The novel is based on a true story (which/that) her mother told her. 3 My son lent me this book, which I'm trying to finish before he gets back. 4 I know the woman (who's) giving tonight's book reading. 5 Did you read that paperback (which/that) I lent (to) you last week? 6 Jacqueline Wilson is a writer whose books are read by millions of young girls all over the world.

4C Very funny!

1 c
2 1 because 2 Even though 3 instead of 4 despite 5 Nevertheless, 6 since
3 1 a 2 b 3 c 4 b 5 a
4 2 As 3 Even though 4 whereas 5 instead of 6 Apart from

4D How was your day?

1 2 driving; crazy 3 killing 4 nightmare 5 forever 6 dying; drink
2 2 a ton 3 over the moon 4 scared stiff 5 out of my mind 6 speechless
3a 2 I can imagine 3 He would say that, wouldn't he? 4 That is fantastic news. 5 to be honest 6 I bet you were!
 b b I bet you were! c He would say that, wouldn't he? d to be honest e That is fantastic news! f I can imagine.

5A Nature's best

1 1 Keeping a pet can be **time-consuming** but it can also be **rewarding** if you do it well. 2 Rats can seem **weird** pets but the British first started keeping them over 150 years ago. 3 Pet smuggling can be **lucrative** for criminals. 4 Monkeys are fortunately **rare** as pets because they need constant attention and can be **fierce** towards people. 5 Children are usually **enthusiastic** about pets for the first few months but many will lose interest in their animals after this.
2 2 unsuitable 3 affectionate 4 harmless 5 destructive 6 faithful
3a 2 c 3 d 4 a 5 b
 b 1 no harder than 2 just as easy 4 nearly as expensive as 5 only slightly cheaper 7 not nearly as friendly as 8 nowhere near as hard work as 9 a great deal easier 10 considerably more dangerous than
4 2 nearly 3 than 4 cute 5 far 6 much 7 less 8 quite 9 no
5 2 not nearly as expensive as 3 as near as interesting as 4 are a great deal larger 5 a little easier to 6 as intelligent as
6 2 Rabbit's fur is as **soft** as feathers. 3 There are thousands more leopards in the world **than** tigers.

Answer Key

4 Bee stings are a lot **more** painful than mosquito bites. 5 The number of wild tigers is getting smaller and smaller each year. 6 Spiders are **far** more frightening than ants.

5B Royal treasures

1 1 catch up on 2 fit in with; go ahead 3 pass by; put you out 4 talk me into; packed out

2 2 If you need me, I'll be sitting outside in the garden. 3 They're **coming** to lay a new lawn this afternoon. 4 I'm going to **buy** some fresh herbs. 5 The castle doesn't **open** until ten. 6 The pollen **will probably** make me sneeze. 7 I'll **water** the plants if you like. 8 I imagine we'll **be** working in the garden all weekend.

3 A b 4 B Present Simple c 5 C Present Continuous d 3 D Future Continuous e 8 f 2 E *will* g 7 h 6

4 2 going to have 3 'll be seeing 4 'm giving 5 'll find 6 Are you going to 7 'll use 8 'll be watching 9 'll be waiting 10 have

5 2 will probably get 3 Will you be able 4 'm going 5 'll see 6 won't be coming 7 goes 8 'll be leaving 9 gets 10 miss 11 'll be asking

6 2 'll be thinking 3 'll be meeting 4 will soon be wondering 5 will be flying 6 Will you be staying

5C The nature of cities

1 B

2 2 DS 3 F 4 T 5 F 6 F

3a 2 lurk 3 fowl 4 lunge 5 giant 6 unwary
 b a loiter b lunge c unwary d giant e fowl f lurk

5D Carbon footprints

1 2 inevitable; wasteful 3 unsustainable 4 disturbing; justifiable 5 ethical; damaging

2 2 d 3 c 4 f 5 e 6 a

3 2 Well, some people would 3 Yes, but then again 4 One argument in favour of 5 I've never really thought about 6 That's an interesting 7 I don't think it's right 8 Maybe, but I just don't 9 No, that's not what I

6A Codes of conduct

1 2 e 3 d 4 c 5 a 6 g 7 h 8 b 9 j 10 f

2 2 trying 3 annoying 4 wasting 5 apologising 6 Chatting 7 going 8 being 9 enjoying

3 2 Despite living here, I don't understand British humour. 3 People don't like you standing too close in some cultures. / People in some cultures don't like you standing too close. 4 Eating in restaurants is expensive in some countries. 5 I try to avoid answering direct questions. 6 The English hate being asked how much they earn.

4 2 Smoking 3 Talking about the weather 4 Being late 5 Shaking hands 6 Speaking loudly 7 Watching soap operas 8 Complaining

5 1 barking 2 Feeling 3 ✓ 4 I noticed 5 ✓ 6 taking

6B Rebel!

1 2 big-headed 3 strong-willed 4 level-headed 5 self-centred 6 narrow-minded 7 laid-back 8 self-conscious 9 absent-minded

2 2 They are bound to prefer Emma. 3 ✓ 4 I doubt if Steve will apply for the job. 5 She's unlikely to have another interview. 6 ✓ 7 I can't imagine they will/would choose her for the job. 8 ✓

3 2 bound to 3 may well 4 doubt 5 unlikely 6 can't imagine 7 dare say 8 couldn't

4 2 don't suppose she will mind 3 doubt he will arrive / be arriving 4 can't imagine it will be cold 5 likely to forget

5a 2 I can't imagine what will happen in the next episode of *High Street*. 3 I don't suppose Bruce will get back from lunch before two. 4 It's unlikely (that) Ellie will invite us to her party now. 5 I dare say (that) Jamie will be playing computer games again, as usual.
 b a 4 b 5 c 2 d 3 e 1

6C Dress code

1 no

2 1 a 2 b 3 a 4 a 5 b 6 a 7 b 8 a

3 2 F 3 T 4 F 5 T 6 DS 7 T 8 DS

6D Sorry to interrupt ...

1 2 Sorry to disturb you. 3 Can I have **a** word? 4 Sorry **to** bother you, but have you got a minute? 5 I was wondering if I could see you for a moment.

2 2 I'm really up against it at the moment. 3 Can I have a word? 4 I'm a bit tied up just now. 5 Sorry to bother you, but have you got a minute? 6 Sorry, this isn't a good time. 7 Sorry to disturb you. 8 I'm rather pushed for time at the moment. 9 I was wondering if I could see you for a moment. 10 I'm really rather busy.

3 2 Are you going to 3 I'll be working 4 I'll probably meet 5 is coming 6 I'll 7 goes 8 won't have to

7A At the airport

1 2 doubt 3 realises 4 deserves 5 trusts 6 recognise 7 suit 8 involve 9 respect

2a 2 d 3 a 4 f 5 c 6 b
 b b 1 c 5 d 3 e 4 f 2

3 2 've been doing 3 is starting 4 'm doing 5 have to 6 was flying 7 had brought 8 arrived 9 'm thinking 10 was talking 11 seemed 12 suspect

4 2 Did you see; 'm thinking 3 's / has been behaving; Do you think 4 have had; 'm thinking 5 saw; was having

7B Showpiece of China

1 2 production 3 economies 4 Industrial 5 Manufacturers 6 produce 7 distribution 8 development 9 environmentalists 10 economists

2 1 b 2 a 3 d 4 c 5 e 6 f 7 h 8 g

3 2 have been decorating. 3 has been falling since 2000. 4 has been driving for three hours / since 6 o'clock. 5 has been rising since 1970. 6 has been snowing for six hours.

4 2a has he phoned b have been phoning 3a have been learning b Have you ever learnt 4a Have you been painting? b have painted 5a have replied b have been replying 6a has been trying b have tried

Answer Key

7C Life online

1 2 mispronounce 3 ex-colleague
   4 pro-government
   5 underqualified 6 non-smoker
   7 post-war
2 2 self- 3 anti- 4 over 5 multi-
3 2 F 3 DS 4 T 5 T 6 DS 7 T

7D You're breaking up

1 2 contract 3 touchscreen
   4 pay-as-you-go 5 cut off
   6 reception 7 smartphone
   8 landline 9 ringtone
2 2 b 3 a 4 c 5 a
3 2 breaking up 3 catch any of that
   4 signal isn't very good 5 keep
   losing 6 got cut off 7 my battery
   8 calling you 9 phone you back
   10 a bit of a delay 11 on your
   landline 12 you'll have to speak up
   13 my battery's about to

8A I'm broke

1 2 rate 3 repay 4 loan 5 on
   6 of 7 cash 8 on 9 off 10 in
2 1 c 2 a;c 3 a;b 4 a 5 b 6 c
3 Hi Jo,
   I've been at college a month now, but
   it feels like I've been here all my life!
   Hard work, but I'm enjoying it. I
   just wish I ~~have~~ had more money. I
   always seem to be overdrawn. At the
   moment I'm broke, but luckily it's
   nearly time for my parents ~~sending~~
   to send me my monthly cheque. If
   only they **would** send / **sent** one every
   week!
   Anyway, how are you? How's the
   new job? I wish you ~~be~~ were here
   instead. It would be much more
   fun! If only there was a direct train
   service, you could come down more
   often. Anyway, it's about time I ~~do~~
   did some work. I haven't done any
   for two days.
   I hope ~~you'd~~ you/you'll email me
   soon.
4 2 found 3 will leave 4 had
   5 could buy

8B Every little helps

1 2 up 3 off 4 back 5 down
   6 out 7 down 8 off 9 to 10 off
2 2 'd set 3 have booked 4 'd gone
   5 hadn't decided 6 have told
3 2 'd waited 3 've known
   4 have given up 5 hadn't listened
   6 'd worked 7 have become
   8 'd learned 9 have taken
   10 'd spent

4a 2 e 3 a 4 d 5 f 6 b
 b a 5 b 3 c 1 d 6 e 4 f 2
5 1 I wish I'd learned to dance. 2 You
   shouldn't have parked here.
   3 I wish I hadn't bought so much.
   4 I should have looked at the weather
   forecast.

8C A bit extra

1 a
2 2 D 3 B 4 A 5 D 6 E 7 B
   8 B 9 D
3 2 reductions – discounts 3 pay –
   financial reward 4 the be-all and
   end-all – the most important
   consideration 5 extra – additional
   6 appreciated – valued 7 employees
   – workers 8 leave – holiday

8D I didn't realise

1 2 d 3 c 4 b 5 f 6 a
2 a have put it down 2 returning
   your call b you'd phoned until
   a few minutes ago 3 I'm so
   late c for some reason 4 what I
   said yesterday d to upset you
3 2 She grew up in Long Island, which
   is an hour away from New York.
   3 She is a best-selling writer,
   whose books are read all over the
   world. 4 Her books, which deal
   with teenage issues and family
   problems, have been described as
   'soap operas'. 5 She gets a lot of
   ideas for her books from her friends,
   who tell her all the gossip in the
   small town they live in. 6 She
   spends more than 100 days a year
   giving readings, which she believes
   helps to sell her books.

9A The silver screen

1 2 c 3 a 4 a 5 b 6 c 7 a 8 c
   9 b 10 a 11 b 12 b
2 2 had fallen 3 were still being
   produced 4 was released 5 had
   been taken 6 to fall 7 was being
   invested 8 were produced 9 left
   10 were provided 11 be seen
   12 are increasing
3 2 is being shot in the UK, Turkey and
   China. 3 has been dubbed into 12
   languages. 4 is included 5 was
   being shown on all three screens.
   6 is going to be directed by Peter
   Jackson.
4 2 This film is famous for being made
   in less than a month. 3 Cartoons
   used to be drawn by hand but
   nowadays they are drawn on
   computers. 4 Harry Potter and the

Deathly Hallows was the last film
based/to be based on J K Rowling's
best-selling novels. 5 The American
actors spent weeks being trained in
British pronunciation. 6 Shooting
of the film will be delayed for three
months for legal reasons. 7 I prefer
films that are/have been subtitled
rather than dubbed. 8 If it were less
expensive, more films would be made
in the UK.

9B What was it like?

1 2 moving 3 believable 4 overrated
   5 hilarious 6 underrated
   7 gripping 8 realistic
   9 predictable 10 weird
2 2 like 3 such 4 so 5 like
   6 so 7 such a 8 like 9 many
   10 Such as 11 like 12 such
   13 so 14 as 15 like 16 like
3 2 like old leather 3 As his manager
   4 like/such as nursing 5 as a waiter
   6 like the Queen 7 as it always is
   8 as a substitute
4a 2 such an 3 such a 4 so 5 such a
   6 So 7 so 8 so
 b 2 so underrated 3 was so
   predictable, I left before the end.
   4 such an unbelievable ending, I
   couldn't stop laughing. 5 credit
   rating is so bad, I can't get a loan
   from anyone.

9C Is it art?

1 2 E 3 D 4 F 5 A
2 b clear c play d light e poor
   f show
3a 2 show 3 play 4 poor 5 light
   6 clear
 b b light c poor d letter(s)
   e show f clear

9D It's up to you

1a 2 Are you doing anything interesting
   this weekend? 3 Do you fancy
   going to see that new French film?
   4 Do you feel like eating out or
   getting a take-away? 5 I thought we
   could give that new Indian restaurant
   a try on Saturday.
 b b I **don't** really mind. It's up to you.
   c I'd rather give spicy food a miss, if
   you don't mind. d I'm going to bed
   early. Some other **time**, perhaps?
   e Well, I wouldn't mind **going** to the
   sales on Saturday morning.
 c 2 e 3 a 4 b 5 c
2 2 got anything 3 'm not bothered
   either 4 up to going 5 give it a
   miss 6 fancy seeing

Answer Key

3 2 I don't really feel up to going to the gym today. 3 I'm not bothered either way. 4 Have you got anything on next Friday? 5 Do you fancy seeing my brother's band play live? 6 I'd rather give it a miss, if you don't mind.

10A How practical are you?

1 2 put in; burglar alarm 3 replacing; locks 4 bedroom; redecorated 5 cut; grass 6 put up; wall 7 roof; repaired; checked; leaks 8 rugs; dry-cleaned

2 2 b 3 c 4 c 5 a 6 c 7 b 8 a 9 c 10 a 11 b

3 2 Roger had a burglar alarm put in for him. 3 Martha is going to put up some shelves herself. 4 Roger had his car serviced at a garage. 5 Martha has fixed a leak in her bathroom herself. 6 Martha cuts the grass herself.

4 2 have; had 3 haven't had 4 got; get/have 5 get 6 have/get 7 are having/are getting 8 didn't get 9 get/have

10B The youth of today

1 2 b 3 a 4 c 5 b 6 a 7 c 8 c 9 b 10 a

2 2 have got 3 likes 4 costs 5 knows; thinks 6 carries 7 eat/eats 8 is

3 2 no key 3 none of the accused 4 no help 5 no trains 6 None of the food

4 2 cousins 3 no 4 team 5 Neither 6 None of 7 All 8 landlord 9 both of 10 Everyone

5 2 every 3 none of 4 no one 5 Everything 6 all 7 neither 8 no 9 everyone

10C Battle of the sexes

1a b ended c polite d place e forward f tags g loving

b 2 gossip-loving 3 question tags 4 straightforward 5 super-polite 6 workplace 7 open-ended

2 2 T 3 F 4 T 5 T 6 T

10D I did tell you!

1a 2 d 3 c 4 f 5 a 6 e

b 2 The thing that drives me mad about our area is the litter. 3 One thing I love about cutting grass is the wonderful smell. 4 The thing I hate about weekends is Sunday evenings. 5 What I admire about flight attendants is that they're always so cheerful. 6 One thing that impresses me about Simon is his determination.

2 2 kids nowadays is that they're so rude. 3 having my hair done is that it takes ages. 4 makes me think about retiring is my health. 5 don't enjoy about Hollywood films is that they're so predictable. 6 annoys me about these trousers is that they have to be dry-cleaned.

3 2 Our bathroom had to **be** redecorated after the flood. 3 A statement is going **to** be made at midday tomorrow. 4 The boiler had to be fixed when it ~~was broken~~ broke down. 5 I paid £50, so I think it was **a** rip off. 6 They ~~were~~ put in a burglar alarm last week.

11A Meeting up

1a 2 on the go 3 a living 4 redundant 5 work 6 a project 7 a living 8 work 9 get 10 a talk

b 2 redundant 3 on the go 4 freelance 5 out of work 6 living

2 2 have found 3 be learning 4 be living 5 have retired 6 be driving 7 be making 8 'll have

3 2 will buy / will be buying 3 will have invented 4 won't eat / won't be eating 5 will live / will be living 6 will have found 7 will have / will be having 8 will have landed 9 will have / will be having 10 will be living

11B Going into business

1 2 a 3 c 4 b 5 a 6 b 7 c 8 a 9 a 10 b 11 c 12 c

2a 2 how much research I did/had done 3 I was going to invest 4 would be advertising for staff 5 I had found a suitable location for the café 6 I had to / must write a business plan before we went any further

b b "I've talked to over 600 people in the town …" c "There'll be three investors …" d "I've found the perfect spot …" e "I'll have it done by tomorrow!"

3 2 if her husband could find 3 her son not to advertise 4 why his colleagues closed down/had closed down 5 If Paula would come/go to the meeting with her 6 to get back to the client

11C The coffee shop

1 b

2 1 T 2 F 3 T 4 F 5 DS 6 DS

3 2 He threatened to close coffee houses down. 3 His people refused to obey him. 4 The article points out that the internet and coffee houses were similar in many ways. 5 People used to invite friends to go to a coffee house and discuss politics.

11D Advertising works

1a 2 leaflets 3 samples 4 product 5 media 6 marketing 7 billboard 8 launch

b 2 publicity 3 budget 4 campaign 5 press 6 design

2 2 The main problem with that 3 How about 4 Yes, that could work 5 I'd rather we didn't 6 So am I right in thinking that 7 Why don't we try and 8 Yes, that makes sense 9 I'm not sure that's such a good idea 10 So are you saying that 11 One thing we could do 12 it's worth a try 13 Maybe we should avoid 14 Can we just go over this again?

12A Where's my mobile?

1a 2 stressed out 3 bug 4 crazy 5 chill out 6 telly 7 trendy 8 mate 9 Hang on a sec 10 quid

b 1 chucking out 2 guy 3 fancy him 4 a hassle 5 pretty 6 messed it up 7 pop into 8 loo

2 2 I think they must be planning to move house. 3 Nikki must have been crying. 4 You can't have lost your passport. 5 He can't be much more than ten. 6 He may be going out later. 7 That might be Tom at the door. 8 He could have forgotten about it.

3 1 must have been 2 may have built 3 can't have carried 4 might have used 5 must have cut 6 could have destroyed 7 couldn't have escaped

12B A great inheritance

1 2 somewhere in the region of 3 tiny 4 or so 5 -odd 6 vast 7 in excess 8 ish 9 give or take 10 roughly

2 2 a 3 b 4 a 5 c 6 a

3 2 would have 3 didn't need to get 4 could have 5 was able to get on 6 shouldn't have 7 needn't have

4 2 b 3 f 4 d 5 a 6 c

v

Answer Key

5 2 should have told 3 would have sent 4 was able to swim 5 needn't have prepared 6 didn't need to say

12C Spooky!
1 2 d 3 e 4 b 5 f 6 c
2 1 T 2 F 3 T 4 DS 5 T 6 T
3 2 a far cry from 3 take with a pinch of salt 4 keep an eye out 5 in the middle of nowhere

Reading and Writing Portfolio 1
1 a
2 2 i 3 d 4 h 5 g 6 e 7 b 8 c
3a b A Writing a first draft
  c B Writing a final draft
  d D Thinking of ideas and ordering them
b 2 A Writing a first draft
  3 C Checking and correcting the first draft
  4 B Writing a final draft
4 Possible answer:
  2 the demands of being a teacher
  3 qualities of a good teacher
  4 work experience in a local school
  5 places to find more information about careers in teaching
5a playing; the two numbers; teachers; many more
b The job is very hard work and requires you to play many different roles – beyond showing students, say, how to multiply two numbers. A teacher's day never ends with the last lesson of the afternoon. Teachers have to give up personal time for lesson preparation, marking homework, meetings, talking to parents and much more.

Reading and Writing Portfolio 2
1 b
2 2 T 3 F 4 F 5 T 6 T 7 F 8 T
3a 1 so much 2 More and more 3 completely 4 at all 5 indeed 6 only; far 7 absolutely 8 huge 9 themselves 10 even 11 just 12 does
b 1 at all 2 does 3 themselves
4 2 at all 3 far 4 myself 5 just 6 indeed 7 huge 8 even 9 does 10 strongly

Reading and Writing Portfolio 3
1 c
2 2 b 3 b 4 a 5 a 6 c
3 2 zero conditional 3 imperatives 4 modal verbs of possibility 5 should
4 b not to be conspicuous about the valuables you are carrying c like to spread your valuables around your body d may be better to let them take it e aware that your attacker might be stronger than you
5 Possible answers:
2 If you don't have a security system, think about installing one. 3 Try to keep a list of phone numbers you might need in an emergency. 4 You might like to install/consider installing a light outside your home. 5 You should ask a neighbour to look after your house when you're on holiday. 6 Don't leave spare keys outside the house. 7 If there is someone in your house, go to a neighbour and call the police. 8 If you see signs of a break-in, be aware that someone could still be in your house.
6 2 e 3 c 4 d 5 b

Reading and Writing Portfolio 4
1 2 A 3 E 4 B 5 C
2 2 band he was in 3 try to get a record deal 4 Depp to take up acting himself 5 first film 6 made him famous/made him a teenage idol 7 international star 8 Depp's children
3 2 Depp 3 Depp 4 a band 5 *The Kids* 6 Los Angeles 7 in Los Angeles 8 Lori Anne Allison 9 Lori's 10 becoming an actor 11 *A Nightmare on Elm Street* 12 becoming a teenage idol 13 Depp 14 (a film role) came along 15 (starring in) *Edward Scissorhands* 16 after *Edward Scissorhands* 17 Vanessa Paradis 18 (his) film roles
4a 2 c 3 a 4 d 5 e
b 1 1, 4 2 2, 3, 5
5 2 then 3 His 4 this; he 5 them 6 one 7 did
6 2 Unfortunately 3 very likely 4 Sadly 5 suddenly

Reading and Writing Portfolio 5
1 2 e 3 d 4 b 5 c
2 2 c 3 d 4 c 5 a 6 d 7 b 8 d 9 b 10 a
3a 2 begin by looking 3 What this 4 did you 5 let me turn 6 said earlier 7 finish by saying
b b 3 c 7 d 6 e 2 f 4 g 5
4a 2 C 3 B 4 D 5 A 6 B 7 A 8 C
b 2 I said earlier 3 know that leaving 4 want to do today is talk to you about 5 means is that we 6 me turn to 7 begin by looking at 8 me finish by saying

Reading and Writing Portfolio 6
1 2 D 3 E 4 B 5 A
2 1 river; pine; cliffs 2 fish; presents 3 bargain 4 birds 5 warm; friendly
3 2 which/that are 3 which/that is 4 which is 5 which is 6 who are 7 which are 8 which is
4 2 vast 3 ancient 4 fascinating 5 spectacular 6 tiny 7 outstanding 8 delicious 9 delighted 10 unique
5 2 We crossed the river in a small boat, rowed by a man from Dalyan. 3 I saw a turtle swimming in the lake. 4 Kaunos was an important Greek town founded in the 6th century BC. 5 We went for a boat trip organised by the tour company. 6 The Turkish 'eye' is a good-luck charm seen everywhere in the town. 7 I took a photo of my wife bargaining for carpets.
6 2 an ancient 3 spectacular 4 delicious 5 delighted 6 tiny 7 fascinating

Reading and Writing Portfolio 7
1 2 1,400 3 Land's End 4 2001 5 £15 million 6 33% 7 £20 million 8 £10 9 hprice@mailme.com 10 2nd April
2 2 ✗ 3 ✓ 4 ✗ 5 ✓ 6 ✓ 7 ✗ 8 ✓
3 1 a; d 2 b; d 3 a; c
4a 2 Last year's course was on Mondays. 3 We have very low fees for the course. 4 The fees will be increasing next year. 5 but it is often full until 5.00 p.m.

Answer Key

b b 5 c 4 d 3 e 2

Reading and Writing Portfolio 8

1 c

2 2 clothes, DVDs 3 they offer a better deal 4 use value brands; use vouchers; set and keep to a budget 5 staying in more to use home entertainment 6 they are cheap; they give comfort 7 spend less on more things

3a 1 appear to be buying 2 seem to offer 3 tend to be leading 4 tend to look for
 b a less b not always true

4 1 generally speaking; in the main; in most cases 2 such as; like 3 According to; In his view

5 2 appear to be buying 3 seem to be getting 4 tend to suffer 5 appear not to be spending / don't appear to be spending 6 tends to be

6 2 tends 3 Generally 4 Apparently 5 like 6 whole 7 main 8 seem 9 such

Reading and Writing Portfolio 9

1 a R b W c B

2 2 DS 3 T 4 T 5 F 6 F 7 T 8 DS

3 a A b B

4 a Reddit (similarly) features; Additional features include
 b Posts are grouped into; The website is very easy to navigate **c** what I love about Reddit is; one of the main strengths of **d** A downside to; One of the drawbacks of

5 b 2 c 4 d 1

6 2 One of the (main/greatest) strengths 3 is grouped into two sections 4 game features some 5 is quite hard to navigate 6 One of the drawbacks of 7 What I love 8 A downside to

Reading and Writing Portfolio 10

1 Between paragraphs B and C

2 2 b 3 b 4 b 5 c

3 2 Therefore 3 In spite of 4 as well as 5 because of 6 Moreover 7 Alternatively 8 though

4 2 along with; as well as 3 What's more; Moreover 4 as a result of; because of 5 So; Therefore 6 Despite; In spite of 7 On the other hand; Alternatively 8 although; though

5 2 He finds it difficult to get by, despite working full-time. 3 More women in Britain are having children later in their lives because of their careers. 4 You could put in the burglar alarm yourself. Alternatively, you could have it installed by a professional. 5 All the fathers I know work full-time. What's more, many of them work over 45 hours per week. 6 She looked after the children, as well as working full-time.

Reading and Writing Portfolio 11

1a 1 B 2 A
 b b 4 c 2 d 3

2 2 F 3 T 4 T 5 F 6 T 7 T 8 F 9 T

3 2 regarding my enquiries 3 I received (your brochure) 4 I note (from your brochure) 5 Could you clarify …? 6 will not require (payment) 7 In addition 8 We look forward to

4 2 I 3 I 4 I 5 I 6 I 7 F 8 F 9 I

5 2 d 3 e 4 i 5 j 6 h 7 a 8 c 9 f 10 b

6 1 I am writing 2 received 3 Regarding 4 enquiries 5 we don't yet know 6 In addition 7 unfortunately 8 However 9 telephone you 10 you would

Reading and Writing Portfolio 12

1 c

2 2 T 3 T 4 F 5 T 6 DS 7 F 8 T 9 DS 10 T

3a b 5 c 8 d 2 e 3 f 7 g 1 h 6
 b 2 c 3 d 4 h 5 g 6 f 7 b 8 a

4 A who apparently **used to** live next door; I must **be getting** old; a man who I **knew many** years ago; **at university** B we'd already been many years ago; I asked Jamie **if he wanted** to go; he got **scared of** it; had to ask them **to stop** the ride

9A The silver screen

Language Summary 9, Student's Book p147

The cinema VOCABULARY 9.1

1 Choose the correct words to fill in the gaps.

"The film's had rave ¹ _a_ online," I told my husband hopefully.

"I don't care if it's won five Oscars," he replied. "I'm not in the mood for a ² ___ film – I'm just too tired to do all that reading."

"But it was ³ ___ in the place we went on holiday."

"Was it? See if the cinema's showing a ⁴ ___ version."

As you can tell, my husband could never be a film ⁵ ___ . He won't watch films ⁶ ___ over 20 years ago. He actually prefers to watch modern ⁷ ___ of films rather than the originals. He likes to see at least three famous names among the ⁸ ___ . Ideally, he likes films ⁹ ___ in the future and special ¹⁰ ___ are more important than an interesting ¹¹ ___ . He once refused to watch a film of Shakespeare's Richard III because he thought it was a ¹² ___ and he'd missed parts I and II!

1	(a)	reviews	b	criticisms	c	analysis
2	a	dubbed	b	remade	c	subtitled
3	a	shot	b	setting	c	put
4	a	dubbed	b	subtitled	c	foreign
5	a	review	b	critic	c	examiner
6	a	shown	b	aged	c	released
7	a	remakes	b	remade	c	sequels
8	a	performance	b	role	c	cast
9	a	released	b	set	c	shot
10	a	effects	b	images	c	trailers
11	a	plan	b	plot	c	scheme
12	a	soundtrack	b	sequel	c	history

The passive GRAMMAR 9.1

2 Read the article and choose the correct verb forms.

timeline: The British Film Industry

1940s
In the 1940s, cinemas were hugely popular in Britain. In 1946, over 1.4 billion tickets ¹*sold/(were sold)* and throughout the decade, many British films had worldwide success.

1950s
By the late 1950s, televisions were becoming common in British homes. Sales of tickets ²*had fallen/had been fallen* to around 500 million. Many good films ³*were still producing/were still being produced* but more people were staying at home.

1960s
The 1960s was a decade of quality British film-making. In 1962, *Dr No*, the first James Bond film, ⁴*released/was released*, along with the classic *Lawrence of Arabia*. Both films were hugely popular worldwide. By the end of the decade, four of the Best Picture Oscars ⁵*had taken/had been taken* home by British-made films.

1970s & 1980s
Over the next 20 years, the world economy had a significant effect on the film industry all over the world. Audiences continued to ⁶*fall/be fallen* and less and less money ⁷*was investing/was being invested* in film-making. In 1981, only 24 films ⁸*produced/were produced* in Britain and by 1984, tickets sales were down to a record low of 54 million. Many talented people ⁹*left/were left* Britain for Hollywood.

1990s
The 1990s saw a rebirth of British film-making. In films such as the hit romantic comedy *Four Weddings and a Funeral*, the money came from America and the stars and the scripts ¹⁰*provided/were provided* by the British.

2000s & 2010s
Throughout the 2000s, and the early 2010s, the recovery has continued. Going to the cinema is now only one of many ways new films can ¹¹*see/be seen*, of course. However, big Oscar successes such as *Slumdog Millionaire* and *The King's Speech*, along with 3D films, mean audiences ¹²*are increasing/are being increased* again.

45

3 Read the active sentences. Then complete the passive sentences. Use *by* and a noun, or a pronoun <u>only</u> if necessary.

1 The writer based the film on a true story.
   The film *was based on a true story.*

2 They are shooting the new James Bond movie in the UK, Turkey and China.
   The new James Bond movie _____

3 They have dubbed the film into 12 languages.
   The film _____

4 The Blu-ray includes an interview with the director.
   An interview with the director _____ on the Blu-ray.

5 The film was so popular they were showing it on all three screens.
   The film was so popular it _____

6 Peter Jackson is going to direct the next *Tintin* film.
   The next *Tintin* film _____

4 Write the sentences in the passive form.

1 I can't stand / tell / the endings of films before I've seen them.
   I can't stand being told the endings of films before I've seen them.

2 This film is famous for / make / in less than a month.

3 Cartoons used / draw / by hand but nowadays they / draw / on computers.

4 *Harry Potter and the Deathly Hallows* was the last film / base / on J K Rowling's best-selling novels.

5 The American actors spent weeks / train / in British pronunciation.

6 Shooting of the film will / delay / for three months for legal reasons.

7 I prefer films that / subtitle / rather than dubbed.

8 If it were less expensive, more films would / make / in the UK.

9B What was it like?

Entertainment adjectives VOCABULARY 9.2

1 Complete the crossword with adjectives to describe films and books.

A film, book, etc. that …

1 is likely to be remembered. (9)
2 makes you feel sad or emotional. (6)
3 is easy to believe. (10)
4 isn't as good as many people think. (9)
5 is extremely funny. (9)
6 is much better than many people think. (10)
7 is extremely exciting. (8)
8 represents real life. (9)
9 is boring because you can guess the story. (11)
10 is very strange and unusual. (5)

as, *like*, *such as*, *so*, *such* GRAMMAR 9.2

2 Choose the correct words/phrases.

1

JAMES ¹*Like/As* my accountant, what would you advise me to do?

MIKE Well, I usually tell clients ²*like/such* yourself that your first priority is to get out of debt.

JAMES How? I've got ³*so/such* a huge overdraft.

MIKE Well, there are ⁴*as/so* many ways in which you could economise. I mean, sometimes you seem to be spending money ⁵*like/such as* there's no tomorrow.

2

OLLIE I'm ⁶*so/such* tired. I had ⁷*such/such a* bad night's sleep.

ANNA That's not ⁸*like/as* you. What's wrong?

OLLIE There are just so ⁹*many/much* things on my mind at the moment.

ANNA ¹⁰*As/Such as*?

OLLIE Work, money. You know, stuff ¹¹*as/like* that.

3

PAT It's ¹²*such/so* awful weather today, isn't it?

SUMI Yes, it was ¹³*so/such* bright this morning. I didn't think it would rain.

PAT Me neither. I had to use my bag ¹⁴*like/as* an umbrella.

SUMI I haven't seen rain ¹⁵*as/like* this for years.

PAT I know what you mean. August isn't ¹⁶*such as/like* it used to be.

3 Complete the sentences with *as*, *like* or *such as* and a phrase in the box. Sometimes there is more than one answer.

| ~~you know~~ | old leather | nursing | the Queen |
| his manager | a substitute | a waiter | it always is |

1 *As you know*, I'll be away next week.
2 This meat tastes _____.
3 _____ for the past four years, I wouldn't hesitate to recommend him for this job.
4 Careers _____ require a lot of training.
5 In my year off before university I worked _____ in a local restaurant.
6 Her voice is so posh. She speaks _____!
7 Meryl Streep's acting was outstanding in the film, _____.
8 Too many big-budget films end up using special effects _____ for a weak plot.

4 a Complete the sentences with *so* or *such a/an*.

1 The story was *so* slow-moving we fell asleep.
2 I can't understand why he's _____ underrated actor.
3 It was _____ predictable film, I left before the end.
4 The ending was _____ unbelievable, I couldn't stop laughing.
5 I've got _____ bad credit rating, I can't get a loan from anyone.
6 _____ many people just don't care about recycling.
7 I get _____ scared by horror films.
8 They were making _____ much noise, I couldn't hear.

b Change sentences 1–5 in **4a**. Change *so* to *such*, and *such* to *so*, and make any other changes necessary.

1 It was *such a slow-moving story we fell asleep.*
2 I can't understand why he's _____ as an actor.
3 The film _____
4 The film had _____
5 My _____

VOCABULARY AND SKILLS 9C — Is it art?

1 Read the article. Which paragraph:

1 describes Esref's background? **B**
2 explains how he is able to paint? ___
3 describes how he learned about painting? ___
4 mentions a job he once did? ___
5 mentions where Esref lives now? ___

Homonyms VOCABULARY 9.3

2 Match words 1–6 in the article to a–f.

a _letter_ : a written message
b _____ : obvious
c _____ : spend time doing something enjoyable, like a game
d _____ : the brightness from the sun, fire, etc. that allows us to see things
e _____ : having little money
f _____ : prove that something is true

3 a Fill in the gaps with words 1–6 from the article. In these sentences, the words have a different meaning.

1 'Mum' and 'dad' are examples of words that begin and end with the same _letter_ .
2 Have you ever been to a fashion _____ ?
3 I've seen both the _____ and the film.
4 That film was ruined by _____ acting.
5 We'd better _____ the barbecue soon.
6 The water was so _____ that you could see the bottom of the lake.

b Match the words in **3a** to definitions a–f.

a _play_ : a piece of writing that is usually performed in a theatre
b _____ : make something start to burn
c _____ : low quality
d _____ : A, B, C, D, etc.
e _____ : an event where things are brought together for people to see
f _____ : transparent or see-through

Seeing things DIFFERENTLY

A Hanging on the wall of painter Esref Armagan's flat in Istanbul is a thank-you ¹**letter** from Bill Clinton. Esref painted the ex-president of the USA and sent the portrait to him. He has never actually read the letter himself – or in fact, ever seen a picture of Bill Clinton. He's blind. He's a blind painter.

B Esref was born in 1953 in a ²**poor** neighbourhood of Istanbul, Turkey. Both of his eyes failed to develop and for children like Esref, there were few opportunities for formal education. Unable to ³**play** with his friends, Esref became interested in drawing, first on walls with nails* and now with paint on canvas*.

C Although it's impossible to say whether he had some vision as a baby, it's ⁴**clear** that he has never been able to see normally. And this makes Esref's work extraordinary. He paints everything from fish, fruit, boats and houses, to portraits of people, but he has never actually seen any of these things. What's more, although his brain has never experienced ⁵**light**, Esref's paintings show shadows and perspective. So, how does he do it?

D Esref has never had any formal training in painting. Instead, he says that he learned about things like colour and shadow from comments by friends. He knows that each object has an important visual quality called colour, so he memorised the typical colours of things. When he first learned about shadow, he remembers, he assumed that something red would have a red shadow!

E Esref's work has been exhibited all over Europe, America and even in China. But his skills as a blind painter have also been the subject of various scientific studies by neurologists. The results raise some interesting questions about how the brain works. When we imagine something we have seen in the past, we use a part of the brain called the visual cortex – the same part that we use when we actually see something. Tests ⁶**show** that Esref uses the visual cortex too, when imagining objects he knows and when drawing. So despite being blind, it seems that Esref can, in his brain, 'see'. And he does this so well that he can transfer these images into his paintings.

F I ask Esref about the birds he loves to paint. He tells me that he used to own a pet shop that sold birds. "You can easily touch them." He pauses and smiles and says, "I love being surrounded by beauty."

*nail = a thin piece of metal with a sharp end, used to join pieces of wood together
*canvas = a strong cloth, used to paint pictures on

9D REAL WORLD — It's up to you

Making and responding to suggestions REAL WORLD 9.1

1 a Make sentences with these words.

1 to / are / tonight / What / up / you ?
   What are you up to tonight?

2 doing / anything / Are / weekend / this / you ?
   _____

3 see that / film / fancy / going / to / new French / Do you ?
   _____

4 out / feel / like / Do / you / a take-away / eating / or getting ?
   _____

5 we / a try / new Indian restaurant / thought / on Saturday / give that / I / could .
   _____

b Correct the mistake in each sentence.

   reading
a I don't feel up to ~~read~~ all those subtitles, actually.
b I really mind not. It's up to you.
c I'd rather to give spicy food a miss, if you don't mind.
d I'm going to bed early. Some other times, perhaps?
e Well, I wouldn't mind go to the sales on Saturday morning.

c Match sentences 1–5 in **1a** to replies a–e in **1b**.

1 _d_   2 ___   3 ___   4 ___   5 ___

2 Complete sentence **b** so it has the same meaning as **a**. Use between two and five words, including the word in brackets.

1 a I think I'd like to go to the gym later.
  b I _wouldn't mind going_ to the gym later. (mind)

2 a Are you doing anything next Friday?
  b Have you _____ on next Friday? (anything)

3 a I don't mind.
  b I _____ way. (bothered)

4 a I'm not in the mood to go to the gym today.
  b I don't really feel _____ to the gym today. (up)

5 a I don't want to go to it.
  b I'd rather _____ , if you don't mind. (miss)

6 a Would you like to see my brother's band in concert?
  b Do you _____ my brother's band play live? (fancy)

3 Complete the conversations with sentences **b** from **2**.

1
CATH ¹ _I wouldn't mind going to the gym later._ How about you?
ROY   ² _____

      What about going for a bike ride?
CATH Or we could play tennis.
ROY   ³ _____

      You choose.
CATH OK. We're playing tennis. Where's your racket?

2
KEN   ⁴ _____

GRACE That's the 14th, isn't it? I don't think so. Why?
KEN   ⁵ _____

GRACE Not again! We saw him a few weeks ago. ⁶ _____

KEN   Oh, go on! It'll be good fun!

> Reading and Writing Portfolio 9 p80

49

10A How practical are you?

Language Summary 10, Student's Book p149

Household jobs VOCABULARY 10.1

1 Clare is showing a friend round her new house. Complete her sentences with verbs and nouns from the boxes.

VERBS
~~replaced~~   ~~serviced~~   dry-cleaned
redecorated   put in   cut   replacing
put up   repaired   checked

NOUNS
~~boiler~~   ~~central heating~~   rugs
leaks   bedroom   burglar alarm
grass   wall   roof   locks

1 The flat's lovely and warm. The _boiler_ was _replaced_ recently and apparently they _serviced_ the _central heating_ at the same time.

2 I don't think we'll need to _____ a _____. There is very little crime in this area.

3 But we are _____ the _____ on the doors and windows. They're very old.

4 This _____ was recently _____ so it looks fine. But we're going to paint the children's room in a lighter colour.

5 We _____ the _____ last week and the garden looks so much better now.

6 The last family here _____ this _____ between the kitchen and the dining room. I think we're going to take it out again and make a large kitchen that we can eat in.

7 The _____ was _____ recently after it was damaged in a storm. During the rain last week we _____ carefully for _____. But there don't seem to be any.

8 The _____ are being _____ at the moment, so the floors look a little bare.

have/get something done, get someone to do something, do something yourself GRAMMAR 10.1

2 Complete the article with the correct words.

If you watch British TV, you might think the UK is obsessed by DIY. However, a recent survey revealed that just over a half of people under 35 can put up bookshelves ¹___. Instead they usually get their dads ²___ it for them. And when they can't get something ³___ for nothing, the under-35s pay for it. On average they spend over £2,000 a year on ⁴___ jobs done for them. One problem is time. Mark, 27, says, "I work all week, so weekends are my free time. I'd rather pay a decorator than paint my flat ⁵___."

A second issue is confidence. Gina, 24, confesses, "My husband and I tried to ⁶___ some leaking taps ourselves a few years back. We ended up flooding the bathroom and had ⁷___ a plumber to come round on a Sunday!"

Gina also admits to not doing some jobs now because of the cost. "The last time we had our boiler ⁸___, we paid £500 for various 'problems' the engineer found. We're not getting it ⁹___ again until it stops working!"

Modern electronic items are often difficult to repair ¹⁰___. And the cost of repairs reveals another growing trend. Mark tells us, "When my old laptop stopped working, I went to a shop to ¹¹___ it repaired. But the estimate was almost as much as the cost of a new laptop, so I just bought a new one!"

1	(a)	themselves	b	himself	c	itself
2	a	do	b	to do	c	done
3	a	do	b	to do	c	done
4	a	to have	b	have	c	having
5	a	myself	b	herself	c	himself
6	a	have	b	get	c	repair
7	a	to have	b	to get	c	got
8	a	serviced	b	service	c	to service
9	a	do	b	did	c	done
10	a	yourself	b	itself	c	myself
11	a	got	b	have	c	had

3 Martha is practical, but Roger isn't practical at all. Complete the sentences about Martha or Roger.

1 a Martha is decorating her flat herself.
  b Roger is _having his flat decorated_ by professionals.
2 a Martha put a burglar alarm in herself.
  b Roger _____ for him.
3 a Martha _____ herself.
  b Roger is going to have some shelves put up for him.
4 a Martha serviced her car herself.
  b Roger _____ at a garage.
5 a Martha _____ herself.
  b Roger has had a leak in his bathroom fixed for him.
6 a Martha _____ herself.
  b Roger has the grass cut by a gardener.

4 Complete the sentences with the correct form of *have* or *get*. Sometimes both verbs are correct.

1 We _had/got_ the boiler serviced last year, so it should be fine.
2 I _____ just _____ my blood pressure checked and it's a little high.
3 We _____ the car serviced since we bought it. We really should soon.
4 I _____ my husband to look after the children this morning so I could _____ my hair done.
5 Sorry, Miss Noakes. I promise I'll _____ Mr Stone to ring you first thing tomorrow.
6 If I have time, I'll _____ the oil checked.
7 We _____ an alarm put in next week because our neighbours were burgled recently.
8 I _____ anyone to check the tyres last time because I didn't think they needed checking.
9 Before you throw that painting away, why don't you _____ it looked at by an expert?

10B The youth of today

Adjectives for views and behaviour VOCABULARY 10.2

1 Read the opinions about young people. Fill in the gaps. Choose a, b or c.

	a	b	c
1	prejudiced	(b) reasonable	abusive
2	biased	unruly	resentful
3	objective	resentful	biased
4	threatening	reasonable	prejudiced
5	objective	abusive	unfair
6	disciplined	fair	objective
7	unfair	threatening	resentful
8	fair	unruly	biased
9	disciplined	threatening	fair
10	unfair	abusive	objective

What do you think of the ... *younger generation?*

Most kids at our school are ¹ _b_ – they know they're at school and they have to behave. Classes can get a bit ² _____ at times but nothing that ever feels out of control.

It's difficult to stay ³ _____ when you read so much every day about crime and young people. But I try not to be ⁴ _____ and I treat every young person I meet in the same way.

I've never met an ⁵ _____ teenager where I live – they're all fantastically polite. Maybe we are just a bit more strict around here and children are better ⁶ _____ .

My own kids feel quite ⁷ _____ that young people are blamed for everything. I know I'm ⁸ _____ but I tend to agree with them. They're good kids and almost all of their friends are too.

I think the whole of society is more ⁹ _____ these days – everybody seems angry. I know it's ¹⁰ _____ but I'm always suspicious of young people.

Quantifiers GRAMMAR 10.2

2 Fill in the gaps with the verbs in the Present Simple. If both singular and plural verb forms are correct, write both.

1 Both of my parents _enjoy_ (enjoy) babysitting our son.
2 All of the children I teach _____ (have got) a mobile phone.
3 I don't think anyone _____ (like) our boss.
4 Each ticket _____ (cost) £25.
5 Everyone who _____ (know) her _____ (think) she's such a friendly girl.
6 No one _____ (carry) much cash any more.
7 Neither of my children _____ (eat) much meat.
8 None of my jewellery _____ (be) very valuable.

3 Complete the sentences with *no* or *none of the* and these nouns.

| ~~flight attendants~~ | food | help |
| trains | accused | key |

1 _None of the flight attendants_ knew how long we would be delayed.
2 There's _____ for this lock.
3 The newspaper said that _____ said a word during the trial.
4 My boyfriend gave me _____ at all with getting the car serviced.
5 There are _____ from here into London after 11.30 p.m.
6 _____ on this menu is vegetarian.

4 Choose the correct words.

1 (Every)/All of time I do any DIY, I always break something.
2 I don't see either of my *cousin/cousins* very often.
3 The repair made *none of/no* difference to the leaks.
4 In a baseball game, each *team/teams* has nine players.
5 *Not any/Neither* of my nieces calls me 'Aunt'.
6 *No/None of* my suits is clean.
7 *Either/All* of my children can cook.
8 Every *landlord/landlords* I've had has insisted on a deposit.
9 I've seen *each/both of* those films and they're awful.
10 *All/Everyone* in my class wants to work in business.

5 Read about Simon's family and fill in the gaps with these words.

| ~~both~~ | no one | all | every | none of |
| neither | everyone | no | everything |

When I look back on my childhood, I feel a bit ashamed. ¹ _Both_ of my parents worked full-time, but my mum also did absolutely everything at home as well. I remember that ² _____ Saturday night, my dad made a meal, but during the week, ³ _____ us helped much. Certainly ⁴ _____ ever suggested that Mum might need a night off. ⁵ _____ was always spotless in the house and I remember that ⁶ _____ of my friends used to be impressed that our house was so tidy. Nowadays, ⁷ _____ of my parents work any more and there are ⁸ _____ children living in their house. When we're together ⁹ _____ helps with cooking and the clearing up. And Mum ... she's still in charge!

VOCABULARY 10C AND SKILLS

Battle of the sexes

Compound nouns and adjectives VOCABULARY 10.3

1 a Complete the words to make compound nouns/adjectives with meanings a–g.

| ~~spread~~ | forward | ended | tags |
| loving | place | polite | |

a wide _spread_ : existing in many places

b open-_____ : being able to finish in several ways

c super-_____ : very careful not to be rude

d work_____ : where people do their jobs

e straight_____ : easy to understand

f question_____ : 'aren't we?', 'do they?', etc.

g gossip-_____ : enjoying conversation about other people's private lives

b Read the article. Fill in the gaps with the compound nouns/adjectives in **1a**.

2 Read the article again. Are these sentences true (T) or false (F)?

1 [F] The article is mainly for women.
2 [ ] In general, men talk more than women.
3 [ ] According to research, women make politer requests than men.
4 [ ] Women are less likely than men to interrupt.
5 [ ] Talking a lot can be both good and bad for your career.
6 [ ] The article encourages men to be more sensitive about interrupting.

He said, she said …

Do men and women really communicate differently? Lucy Charlton researched some of the [1] _widespread_ beliefs about the differences between men and women and has some advice for all of us.

Do women really talk more than men?

The stereotype is that [2]_____ women do talk more. However, the truth is quite the opposite. In mixed-sex groups, men often spend more time talking than women. They also tend to start more conversations.

Are there differences in the way men and women use language?

Several studies have attempted to show that women tend to be 'softer' than men in their requests and statements. For instance, they investigated if women are more likely to use phrases like "Don't you think … ?" before statements or [3]_____ at the end of sentences. However, the results always show that there are very few differences.

Which sex interrupts more?

This question is much more [4]_____. Research clearly shows that men are more likely to interrupt than women, and women are also more likely to be interrupted than men. What's more, women actually allow themselves to be interrupted more than men.

Does it matter?

In short, yes. Research indicates that:

* people who talk the most are often seen negatively as controlling conversations. However, in decision-making groups, they also tend to become the leaders.

* both males and females who use more direct language are perceived as more intelligent and often more able. Conversely, people see users of [5]_____ language as less powerful.

What can we do about it?

We need to look at achieving a balance in the behaviour of men and women that will help both sexes to get their message across.

* Men need to be more conscious about how much they speak in relation to women at home and in the [6]_____, so that they are not seen as too dominant.

* Both sexes should avoid overusing 'soft' expressions and [7]_____ questions such as "How's the project going?" Instead, use more closed questions such as "When will the next stage be complete?"

* Rather than interrupting more often, and becoming more like men, women should concentrate on stopping themselves from being interrupted. Simple strategies such as insisting on finishing your point will help.

10D I did tell you!

Adding emphasis REAL WORLD 10.1

1 a Match the beginnings and ends of the sentences.

1 What depresses me about living …
2 The thing I hate about …
3 One thing I love about cutting …
4 The thing that drives me …
5 One thing that impresses me about Simon …
6 What I admire about flight attendants …

a is his determination.
b in London is the traffic.
c grass is the wonderful smell.
d weekends is Sunday evenings.
e is that they're always so cheerful.
f mad about our area is the litter.

b Complete the conversations with the sentences in **1a**.

1 A _What depresses me about living in London is the traffic._
  B You should try cycling more.
2 A _____
  B We've got the same problem where we live.
3 A _____
  B Yes, it's so fresh, isn't it?
4 A _____
  B Me too. It's that thought of work the next day, isn't it?
5 A _____
  B Yes, they never seem to get annoyed.
6 A _____
  B Yes, he's always been like that.

2 Complete the second sentence so it has the same meaning as the first.

1 I hate DIY because I can't do it!
  The thing _I hate about DIY is that I can't do it!_

2 Kids nowadays upset me because they're so rude.
  What upsets me about _____

3 I can't stand having my hair done because it takes ages.
  What I can't stand about _____

4 My health makes me think about retiring.
  One thing that _____

5 One reason I don't enjoy Hollywood films is that they're so predictable.
  One thing I _____

6 These trousers annoy me because they have to be dry-cleaned.
  The thing that _____

Review: the passive

3 Correct the mistake in each sentence.

                              be
1 He was the first actor to ~~been~~ awarded the prize.
2 Our bathroom had to redecorated after the flood.
3 A statement is going be made at midday tomorrow.
4 The boiler had to be fixed when it was broken down.
5 I paid £50, so I think I was rip off.
6 They were put in a burglar alarm last week.

Reading and Writing Portfolio 10 p82

11A Meeting up

Language Summary 11, Student's Book p152

Work collocations VOCABULARY 11.1

1 a Simon and Ian are at an office party. Complete the conversation with these words.

~~freelance~~   work (x2)   a living (x2)   a talk
get   a project   redundant   on the go

SIMON Hi. I didn't know you worked for this company.
IAN Well, I work ¹ _freelance_ rather than for any one company. But I'm doing something for them at the moment, yes.
SIMON Do you prefer working for lots of different companies?
IAN Well, it means I'm ² _____ most of the time, which keeps life interesting. What are you doing for ³ _____ these days?
SIMON I used to work here, as you know, which is why I'm at this party. After that I worked at a small printing company, but then I was made ⁴ _____ last year.
IAN So are you still out of ⁵ _____ ?
SIMON No, I'm working on ⁶ _____ for homeless people, which the local government has set up. Completely different to what I used to do.
IAN That's fantastic. Do you actually make ⁷ _____ from it or is it unpaid?
SIMON Yes, it does pay reasonably well and I really enjoy it. Do you have a lot of ⁸ _____ on at the moment?
IAN I do, but I've just got back from holiday, so I'm finding it hard to ⁹ _____ down to work again.
SIMON I know the feeling well! I have to give ¹⁰ _____ at a conference on Friday and I haven't even started thinking about it!

b Find words and phrases in **1a** which mean:

1 work completed over a period of time:
a project

2 lose your job because your employer doesn't need you any more:
be made _____

3 be busy:
_to be_ _____

4 work for different organisations:
work _____

5 be unemployed:
_be_ _____

6 earn money:
make a _____

Describing future events; Future Perfect GRAMMAR 11.1

2 Eight people were asked what they hope to have achieved in ten years' time. Choose the correct verb form.

1 I'm sure I'll *become*/(*have become*) a famous footballer.
Darren, 14

2 Hopefully, I'll *be finding*/*have found* my ideal job by then.
Anna, 23

3 I'll probably still *be learning*/*have learned* English!
Jeanne, 19

4 I hope I won't still *live*/*be living* in this town.
Melanie, 29

5 I hope I'll *have retired*/*be retiring*, if I've saved up enough money!
Ron, 55

6 I'll *be driving*/*have driven* a Ferrari instead of my old hatchback.
Daniel, 32

7 I like to think I'll still *be making*/*have made* a living as an actor.
Julia, 20

8 Perhaps *I'm having*/*I'll have* three children by then.
Conor, 25

3 Complete the article with the correct form of the verb in brackets. Use *will*, the Future Continuous or the Future Perfect.

Is our future perfect?

Our reporter, Matthew Powell, talked to a few local residents to get their views of what life will be like in 2050.

Henry Potts

I don't think we ¹ _'ll be going_ (go) shopping any more, we ² _____ (buy) everything on the Internet. And scientists ³ _____ (invent) some pill that means we ⁴ _____ (not eat) food any more.

Bruce Gibbs

We ⁵ _____ (live) much longer, because scientists ⁶ _____ (find) a cure for most of the serious diseases by then. And women ⁷ _____ (have) babies up until their 70s.

Molly Beckett

I certainly think we ⁸ _____ (land) on Mars by then and ordinary people ⁹ _____ (have) holidays in space. I hope some people ¹⁰ _____ (live) on other planets by then, as it will help the overpopulation problem.

11B Going into business

Business collocations VOCABULARY 11.2

1 Read about Christine's life in business. Fill in the gaps. Choose **a**, **b** or **c**.

	a	b	c
1	out	**up**	down
2	go	work	be
3	imported	extended	exported
4	do	make	have
5	expanded	increased	rose
6	bought	took	had
7	losing	debt	loss
8	close	stop	take away
9	business	work	sale
10	turning	going	facing
11	leading	doing	running
12	sequence	line	chain

A few years ago I set ¹ _up_ a jewellery-making company in Mexico. I used to teach English in Mexico City, and a friend and I decided to return there to ² _____ into business together. At first, it was a great success and we ³ _____ our jewellery to countries throughout Europe. We were beginning to ⁴ _____ a profit and were really pleased, so after a year or two we ⁵ _____ the business and ⁶ _____ over another jewellery business in Guadalajara. However, unfortunately after a couple of years it began to make a ⁷ _____ and we had to ⁸ _____ some of the workshops. Eventually we went out of ⁹ _____ altogether, although we avoided ¹⁰ _____ bankrupt. We have a new project now – ¹¹ _____ a ¹² _____ of pizza restaurants.

Christine

Reported speech GRAMMAR 11.2

2 a Paula is starting a new business. Read what the business adviser at her bank said to her. Then complete Paula's conversation with her friend James.

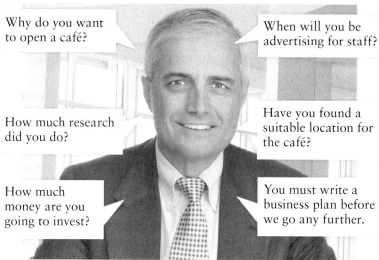

Why do you want to open a café?
When will you be advertising for staff?
How much research did you do?
Have you found a suitable location for the café?
How much money are you going to invest?
You must write a business plan before we go any further.

JAMES Hi. How did the interview with the business adviser go?
PAULA OK, I think, but I'm glad it's over!
JAMES What did he ask you?
PAULA Well, first he asked me ¹ _why I wanted to open a café._
JAMES Oh! What did you say?
PAULA I said because ᵃ**everyone in this town had been hoping for years** that a small café with decent food would open, but it never had.
JAMES And did he ask you about your research?
PAULA Yes, he asked me ² _____ and I told him ᵇ**I'd talked to over 600 people in the town** and also in all the villages around.
JAMES And what else?
PAULA Well he wanted to know how much money ³ _____ and I said that ᶜ**there would be three investors** each putting in twenty thousand.
JAMES As well as him, we hope!
PAULA Yes, exactly. Then he asked me when ⁴ _____ and I said I was already advertising for suitable people.
JAMES Anything else?
PAULA Yes, he asked if ⁵ _____ for the café.
JAMES OK.
PAULA I told him ᵈ**I'd found the perfect spot** on the High Street, but then he said ⁶ _____ before we went any further. I said ᵉ**I'd have it done by tomorrow!**

b Look at a–e in bold in **2a**. Then write what Paula said to the business adviser in direct speech.

a _"Everyone in this town has been hoping for years_ that a small café with decent food would open, _but it never has."_
b _____
c _____
d _____
e _____

3 Complete sentence **b** so that it has the same meaning as sentence **a**.

1 a "What are you going to call the business?" she asked Tim.
   b She asked _Tim what he was going to call_ the business.

2 a "Can you find an interior designer?" she asked her husband.
   b She wanted to know _____ an interior designer.

3 a "Don't advertise in *The Daily Star*," she told her son.
   b She told _____ in *The Daily Star*.

4 a "Why did you close down the branch?" Will asked his colleagues.
   b Will wanted to know _____ the branch.

5 a "Will you come with me to the meeting, Paula?" Julia wanted to know.
   b Julia wanted to know _____ the meeting with her.

6 a "Get back to this client immediately, please," he told Mike.
   b He told Mike _____ immediately.

VOCABULARY AND SKILLS 11C: The coffee shop

Reading

1 Read the article quickly and complete this sentence.

The title of the article is *The Internet in a cup* because:

a nowadays you can log on to the Internet in a coffee shop.

b coffee shops in the past used to have the same function as the Internet today.

c an early form of Internet technology was first used in coffee shops.

2 Read the article again. Are these sentences true (T), false (F) or the article doesn't say (DS)?

1 ☐ Coffee houses acted as a source of information in the days before newspapers.

2 ☐ Only serious information tended to be discussed in coffee houses.

3 ☐ Coffee houses were sometimes seen as a threat to governments.

4 ☐ Most people tended to go to only one coffee house.

5 ☐ Coffee was not as expensive as alcohol.

6 ☐ Turkey was the first country where coffee was drunk.

Verb patterns (2): reporting verbs VOCABULARY 11.3

3 Make sentences with these words.

1 King Charles II blame / coffee houses / spread political unrest.

   King Charles II blamed coffee houses for spreading political unrest.

2 He threatened / close / coffee houses down.

3 His people refused / obey him.

4 The article points out / the Internet and coffee houses / be / similar in many ways.

5 People used to invite / friends / go to a coffee house and discuss politics.

The Internet in a cup

Where do you go when you want to know the latest business news or keep up with the latest scientific and technological developments? Today the answer is obvious: go online. Three hundred years ago, the answer was just as easy. You went to a coffee shop, or coffee house as it was called then. Collectively, Europe's interconnected web of coffee houses formed the Internet of the 17th century.

Like today's websites, coffee houses were lively and often unreliable sources of information. News and gossip were regularly passed between them and runners would go around reporting major events such as the outbreak of a war or the death of someone important. Coffee houses were also popular places to have political discussions, which is why King Charles II tried, unsuccessfully, to have London's coffee houses closed down in 1675.

In the days before street numbering or regular postal services it became common practice to use a London coffee house as a postal address and regular customers would pop in to see if there was any post for them while they were checking up on the latest news. Most people frequented several coffee houses, as different locations attracted different people: Will's in Covent Garden was a popular venue for writers, the Westminster coffee houses attracted the politicians, businessmen went to the Royal Exchange and financiers to Lloyd's.

The drink that fuelled this network originated in Ethiopia, where the beans used to be chewed, rather than drunk. The first coffee house opened in 1475 in Istanbul, Turkey, a place where coffee was so important that it was legal for a woman to divorce her husband if he could not supply her with enough of the drink. A hundred years later, a coffee house was opened in Vienna and they spread quickly through Europe. The popularity of coffee owed much to the growing middle class, who preferred coffee to alcohol because they believed it stimulated mental activity.

Can the Internet claim to have had as much impact as the coffee houses? Perhaps. What is interesting, though, is how modern coffee shops, different from the old ones in so many other ways, now provide wifi access, so that people can sip their cappuccinos and find out the news of the day, just as they used to.

11D REAL WORLD — Advertising works

Advertising VOCABULARY 11.4

1 a Choose the correct words.

1. The artist designed a great (logo)/slogan.
2. They handed out publicity/leaflets in the shopping centre.
3. They give away free samples/campaigns in the supermarket.
4. They launched the product/budget in October.
5. Their advertising campaign was all over the press/media, except television.
6. The new trainers unexpectedly benefited from viral campaigns/marketing when young people praised them on social networks.
7. I saw a great advert for my favourite shampoo on a billboard/slogan on my way in to work.
8. When is the party to design/launch your new book?

b Match the words you didn't choose in **1a** to these definitions.

1. a short phrase to advertise something: _slogan_
2. the attention someone gets from appearing in newspapers, etc.: _____
3. the amount of money available to spend on advertising: _____
4. a series of advertisements for a product: _____
5. printed media, such as newspapers and magazines: _____
6. make or draw plans for a new product: _____

Discussion language (3) REAL WORLD 11.1

2 Laura, Tim and Steve work for an advertising agency. They are discussing the launch of a new chewing gum. Fill in the gaps with the phrases in the boxes.

A

> ~~I wonder if it would be a good idea~~   I'd rather we didn't
> How about   Yes, that could work   The main problem with that
> So am I right in thinking that

LAURA ¹ _I wonder if it would be a good idea_ to get a famous footballer to launch the product.
TIM ² _____ is that it's been done too often before.
LAURA I suppose so. Let's think. OK. ³ _____ using that runner who won the London Marathon this year instead?
TIM ⁴ _____. What do you think, Steve?
STEVE ⁵ _____ have a sports person at all, to be honest.
LAURA ⁶ _____ you want us to have an actor or singer, or someone? Or not to use a celebrity at all?

B

> So are you saying that   Why don't we try and
> I'm not sure that's such a good idea   Yes, that makes sense

TIM I know. ⁷ _____ advertise it in *Girl Talk*?
STEVE That new teen magazine? ⁸ _____.
LAURA ⁹ _____. That's bought by girls and I thought we were aiming at boys.
STEVE ¹⁰ _____ we don't try to sell this to girls at all?

C

> it's worth a try   Can we just go over this again?
> Maybe we should avoid   One thing we could do

STEVE ¹¹ _____ is give out free samples with a national magazine.
LAURA Well, we may not have enough in the budget, but ¹² _____.
TIM ¹³ _____ using free samples. It's so expensive. What's wrong with the idea of the poster campaign we were discussing?
LAURA OK. ¹⁴ _____ We all agree we need a big campaign, but we don't want to spend too much.

Reading and Writing Portfolio 11 p84

12A Where's my mobile?

Language Summary 12, Student's Book p155

Colloquial words/phrases

VOCABULARY 12.1

1 a Replace the words/phrases in bold with the colloquial words/phrases in the box.

~~What's up?~~	trendy	quid
hang on a sec	bug	
stressed out	crazy	
chill out	mate	telly

What's up?

LAURA ¹**What's the matter?** You look tired. Another late night?

NICOLE No, it's worse than that. I'm really ²**worried and anxious** about work. Well, about my boss, really.

LAURA Not again! You really shouldn't let him ³**annoy** you so much.

NICOLE I know. You're going to tell me I'm ⁴**stupid**.

LAURA Yes, I am. You should just ⁵**relax** more. He's not worth it.

NICOLE I know. Maybe I'll just go home and watch ⁶**television**.

LAURA Oh no you won't! Let's go to that ⁷**fashionable** new bar that's just opened.

NICOLE Oh, Laura, you're such a good ⁸**friend**, you know!

LAURA ⁹**Wait a moment**. Not so good, actually. I haven't got any cash on me.

NICOLE No problem. I've got a few ¹⁰**pounds**.

b Replace the words in bold with these words and phrases.

| loo | messed it up | a hassle | pretty |
| guy | pop into | fancy him | chucking out |

ALFIE Hi, Jess. What are you doing?

JESS I'm ¹**throwing away** all my old photos and letters.

ALFIE So who's this ²**man** here?

JESS Oh, that's Jamie. I used to ³**find him really attractive** when I was about 14!

ALFIE And what happened to him?

JESS Oh, it became ⁴**complicated** because my sister liked him, too. So I didn't see him again.

ALFIE Well, 14 is ⁵**quite** young to really be in love!

JESS Exactly. How was your driving test?

ALFIE Oh, I ⁶**did it badly** again. I just can't do three-point turns.

JESS Never mind. I'll tell you what – let's ⁷**go to** that new restaurant in Castle Street for a quick lunch. I'll drive!

ALFIE Great. I'll just go to the ⁸**toilet** and then I'm ready.

Modal verbs (2): deduction in the present and the past

GRAMMAR 12.1

2 Make sentences with these words.

1 be / That / brother / must / Diana's / guy
   That guy must be Diana's brother.

2 I / house / to / must / move / they / be / think / planning

3 must / been / crying / Nikki / have

4 lost / can't / passport / You / have / your

5 much / can't / ten / He / than / be / more

6 going / be / may / later / out / He

7 might / Tom / be / That / door / the / at

8 could / He / forgotten / have / it / about

60

3 Read the article. Complete sentence **b** so that it means the same as sentence **a**. Use the word in brackets.

The mystery of Easter Island

Easter Island, famous for its huge stone statues, is over a thousand miles away from its nearest neighbour, in the middle of the Pacific. When Europeans first arrived on Easter Island in the 18th century, they were amazed to find so many statues, many of them unfinished, and so many people dying of starvation.

So what had happened?

1. a It is now believed that there were over 800 statues on Easter Island at one time. (must)
   b There _____ over 800 statues on Easter Island at one time.
2. a Historians think that perhaps the islanders built the statues for protection. (may)
   b The islanders _____ the statues for protection.
3. a The statues were much too heavy for people to carry from one part of the island to another. (can't)
   b The people living there _____ the statues around the island themselves.
4. a It's possible that the islanders used logs to move the statues around the island. (might)
   b The islanders _____ logs to move the statues around the island.
5. a The only way of getting logs was to cut the trees down. (must)
   b The islanders _____ the trees down to get logs for the statues.
6. a Maybe, by cutting the trees down, the islanders destroyed their environment. (could)
   b The islanders _____ their environment by cutting down the trees.
7. a It was impossible for the islanders to escape, because they had no wood left to make boats. (couldn't)
   b The islanders _____ because they had no wood left to make boats.

12B A great inheritance

Vague language expressions VOCABULARY 12.2

1 Read the quotes from three different people. Fill in the gaps with one of the words/phrases/suffixes in the box.

-odd	ish	vast
roughly	~~tons of~~	
somewhere in the region of		
or so	tiny	give or take
in excess		

"We inherited ¹ _tons of_ books from my grandparents when they died. There must have been ² _____ a couple of thousand. We didn't know what to do with them, as we have a ³ _____ flat and no space for them. After a month ⁴ _____ of living with them piled up all around us, we gave them to a charity shop! I just hope they weren't valuable!"

"My dad left me his car when he died, which was strange, because I was the only daughter who couldn't drive. I had to persuade a friend to go and pick the car up for me – my dad used to live 250 ⁵ _____ kilometres away – and then I had a ⁶ _____ amount of lessons – certainly ⁷ _____ of 60. Maybe even more than 70! I still didn't pass my test so in the end I had to sell it. It's a pity – at the moment I have to take a bus and a train to and from work, and with a car I'd get home at six ⁸ _____ instead of at 7.30!"

"I was my aunt's only remaining relative so when she died at about eighty I inherited everything, ⁹ _____ a few items. She had always said she would never part with this particular vase, so I took it home, even though it's really ugly. After ¹⁰ _____ a year, I decided I couldn't live with it any more and took it to be valued. I thought it would be worthless, so I was astonished when they quoted me £2,000. But I still haven't sold it and I still don't like it."

Past forms of modals and related verbs

GRAMMAR 12.2

2 Choose a phrase to complete each sentence.

1 Even if you'd asked me,
   a I shouldn't have helped you.
   (b) I couldn't have helped you.
   c I needn't have helped you.

2 Sorry I'm so late. My meeting went on for hours, but I
   a should have phoned.
   b must have phoned.
   c needn't have phoned.

3 I missed the train yesterday, but fortunately I
   a could get a lift with Joe.
   b was able to get a lift with Joe.
   c could have got a lift with Joe.

4 Thanks very much for the present, but you really
   a shouldn't have.
   b couldn't have.
   c wouldn't have.

5 In that situation, I'm not sure what I
   a needn't have said.
   b should have said.
   c would have said.

6 We walked straight in because we had free tickets and
   a didn't need to pay.
   b should have paid.
   c needn't have paid.

3 Read Jacqui's email. Choose the correct words.

Dear Sam,

It's a shame you ¹(couldn't)/wouldn't come to our party – you ²should have/would have really enjoyed it. Next time we'll make sure we give you more warning!

The last person didn't leave until about 3.00 a.m., but no one stayed overnight so we ³needn't have got/didn't need to get any beds ready, which was a relief. I was very tired this morning, but actually we ⁴could have/would have gone back to bed for a bit because the kids were watching that old film, E.T. (you remember, the one about the alien), on TV. In fact they watched it all the way through, so I ⁵could have got on/was able to get on with some housework, which was good, as the house was such a mess. Actually, I ⁶wouldn't have/shouldn't have spent all that time cleaning it before the party – it was a complete waste of time! I really ⁷couldn't have/needn't have bothered!

Jacqui

4 Match sentences a–f to replies 1–6.

a I haven't got enough money to buy that mp3 player.
b Thanks for lending me the jumper. I've washed it for you.
c Didn't you enjoy your skiing holiday?
d It was fantastic this morning. I had a lie-in.
e Did you manage to get to the bank for me this morning?
f I really enjoyed art lessons when I was at school.

1 _e_ I'm sorry, but I wasn't able to in the end.
2 ___ You needn't have done that.
3 ___ I didn't – I couldn't draw to save my life!
4 ___ Oh, of course, you didn't need to take Jack to school, did you?
5 ___ You should have saved some, shouldn't you?
6 ___ I did, but we could have gone on three summer holidays for the same price!

5 Fill in the gaps with the verbs in the box and the correct form of the verb in brackets.

| needn't | would | didn't need |
| should | ~~could~~ | was able |

1 A What's the matter? You've gone white.
   B That was a lucky escape.
   We could have crashed (crash).

2 A Mum, have you washed my football kit?
   B No, I haven't. If you needed it, you _____ (tell) me yesterday.

3 A It was Bill's 21st birthday yesterday.
   B Why didn't you tell me? I _____ (send) him a card if I'd known.

4 A How on earth did you survive after the boat sank?
   B Luckily, I _____ (swim) to the shore – it wasn't far.

5 A That was a great meal.
   B Thanks, but I _____ (prepare) so much. There was so much food and no one ate a lot.

6 A Did you explain the situation to Fred?
   B No, I _____ (say) anything. He already knew.

VOCABULARY 12C AND SKILLS — Spooky!

Reading

1 Read the article. Fill in gaps 1–6 with sentences a–f.

a ~~You could say that it's 'raining cats and dogs'.~~

b It must have been extremely powerful!

c Personally, I think this story is the most ridiculous of all.

d There have been accounts of frog rain, fish rain, squid rain, worm rain, even alligator rain.

e People reported picking up fish there that weighed up to four kilos.

f Or some people put it down to fine sand being carried from the Sahara desert and falling as a rain shower.

2 Are the sentences true (T), false (F) or the article doesn't say (DS)?

1 ☐ The reasons for some of the 'weird rains' can be explained.

2 ☐ A whirlwind must have dropped the fish on the Indian village.

3 ☐ The fish in Alabama fell down with the rain.

4 ☐ It was proved that the frogs must have been blown over to Greece.

5 ☐ The red rain which fell on India could have been part of a comet.

6 ☐ The writer of the article doesn't really believe he has seen an alien.

Idioms VOCABULARY 12.3

3 Match the underlined phrases in the article to these definitions.

1 completely unexpectedly: _out of the blue_

2 is very different from: _____

3 don't believe them fully: _____

4 watch for something to appear: _____

5 a long way from towns and cities: _____

IT'S RAINING FROGS

As I sit writing this, I glance out of the window. It's pouring down as usual. ¹ _You could say that it's 'raining cats and dogs'._ Not really, of course – it's only a saying. But that's not to say that in many areas around the world it hasn't rained things just as strange – or even stranger! Weird rain is one of the more extraordinary phenomena that is reported from all corners of the globe from time to time. ² _____ The logical explanation for such odd events is that a tornado or strong whirlwind picked up the animals from shallow water and carried them for hundreds of miles before dropping them. However, this has yet to be proved and it can't quite account for all the incidents. A powerful whirlwind might well explain a rain of small fish, but not the ones that fell on a village in India. ³ _____ They had come crashing down on them completely <u>out of the blue</u>. And on an otherwise clear day in Alabama in 1956, in a place <u>in the middle of nowhere</u>, a small dark cloud formed in the sky. When it was overhead, the cloud let go of its contents: rain, catfish, bass and bream – all of the fish alive. The dark cloud then turned to white and disappeared.

And the inhabitants of a city in southern Greece were surprised one morning in 1981 when they woke up to find small green frogs falling from the sky. Weighing just a few grams each, the frogs landed in trees and on the streets. The Greek weather experts came to the conclusion they had been picked up by a strong wind. ⁴ _____ That species of frog was native to North Africa. Other objects can also rain out of the sky. There have been reports of crabs, birds, ice blocks and soft drink cans. Perhaps the most bizarre are the 'rains of blood' which have been reported from all over the world for thousands of years. Most people <u>take</u> these reports <u>with a pinch of salt</u>.
⁵ _____ However, an Indian physicist has recently claimed that particles taken from the red rain showers that fell on Kerala in 2001 could contain microbes from outer space. This is <u>a far cry from</u> the 'sandstorm' theory. He speculates that the particles could be extraterrestrial bacteria adapted to the harsh conditions of space and that the microbes were carried on a comet or meteorite that later broke apart and mixed with the rain clouds above India.

Yeah, right! ⁶ _____ But I'm still going to <u>keep an eye out</u> just in case. Wait a minute … I think I saw something fall past my window. Was that an alien I just saw?

Reading and Writing Portfolio 12 p86

Reading and Writing Portfolio 1

Planning and drafting

Reading an article about learning languages
Writing planning and drafting an article
Review language ability; imperatives

1 Read the article quickly. Choose the best answer.

The article is aimed at:
a people who speak English, but want to learn another language.
b people who want to learn or are learning English.
c people who want to learn a language without going to classes.

Learning a language: *What? Why? How? When?*

If you want to learn a new language, the very first thing to think about is *why*. Are you just fed up with not being able to communicate when on holiday? ¹ _a_ . Or perhaps you're interested in the literature, films or music of a different culture and you know how much it will help to have a knowledge of the language. Whatever your reasons, there is a lot of truth in this old Czech saying.

> *You live a new life for every new language you speak.*
> *If you know only one language, you only live once.*

Assuming you know what and why you want to learn, how are you going to do it? ² _____ And traditional classes are an ideal start for many people. They provide structure, support and an environment where you can practise under the guidance of someone who (usually) has an excellent knowledge of the language. But nowadays there are many more possibilities.

- The web – there are hundreds of websites with exercises including audio and even videos. And many are absolutely free. ³ _____

- Think of all the ways you can use your current interests to learn a language. ⁴ _____ Listen to some songs in the language and look up the lyrics online. Don't expect to understand everything, just enjoy getting used to the language. Love reading? Readers – novels written or adapted especially for language learners – are available for all language levels. And research shows that reading is a highly effective way of improving your language ability.

- Take every opportunity you can to use your language – whether chatting with another language learner or ordering a meal in your local, say Italian, restaurant. The staff in my local hairdresser's are Lebanese and many of them are learning English. Every day they have an 'English hour' when they all speak English to each other, rather than Arabic. ⁵ _____

We all lead busy lives and learning a language takes time. You will have more success if you study regularly, so try to establish a routine. ⁶ _____ Becoming fluent in a language will take years, but learning to get by takes a lot less!

Many people start learning a language and soon give up. "I'm too old," they say. Yes, children do learn languages more quickly than adults, but research has shown that you can learn a language at any age. ⁷ _____

I've also heard people worry about the mistakes they make when learning. Well, relax and laugh about your mistakes and you're much less likely to make them again.

Learning a new language, at any age, is never easy. ⁸ _____ And you'll be amazed by the positive reaction of some people when you say just a few words in their own language. Good luck!

2 Read the article and fill in gaps 1–8 with sentences a–i. There is one extra sentence you don't need.

a ~~Do you need it for a practical reason, such as your job or your studies?~~
b And learning is good for the health of your brain, too.
c But with some work and dedication, you will make progress.
d Try putting a few key words into a search engine and prepare to be amazed by the results!
e It doesn't matter if you haven't got long.
f Or, if you can, join an evening class.
g It's difficult at times, but they have great fun!
h Are you a music lover?
i Well, most people learn best using a variety of methods.

HELP WITH WRITING Planning and drafting an article

3 **a** Look at what the writer of the article wrote at different stages when planning and drafting the article. Match a–d with stages A–D.

a   _C Checking and correcting the first draft_

> If you want to learn a new language, ~~you should~~ think about /\ why.
>   the very first thing to   is
>   communicate
> Are you just fed up with not being able to ~~talk~~ on holiday?

b   _____

> If you want to learn a new language, you should think about why.
> Are you just fed up with not being able to talk on holiday?

c   _____

> If you want to learn a new language, the very first thing to think about is why. Are you just fed up with not being able to communicate on holiday?

d   _____

> 1   intro – ask questions, Czech saying
> 3   routine – do some every day
> 4   don't give up – making mistakes, grammar
> 2   ways of learning – class, WWW, readers

A   Writing a first draft
B   Writing a final draft
C   ~~Checking and correcting the first draft~~
D   Thinking of ideas and ordering them

b What is the best order for doing stages A–D in **3a**?

1   _D Thinking of ideas and ordering them_
2   _____
3   _____
4   _____

4 Read the title of another article and the list of ideas. Put the ideas in a logical order.

Stage 1: Thinking of ideas and ordering them

Thinking about a career in teaching?

- [ ] qualities of a good teacher
- [ ] places to find more information about careers in teaching
- [ ] work experience in a local school
- [ ] the demands of being a teacher
- [1] why you might want to teach

5 **a** Read the first draft of a paragraph from the article in **4**. <u>Underline</u> four more mistakes.

Stages 2 and 3: Writing a first draft; checking and correcting

> Not every person who wants to be a teacher should <u>becomes</u> one. The job is very hard work and requires you playing many different roles – beyond showing students, say, how to multiply the two numbers. A teachers day never ends with the last lesson of the afternoon. Teachers have to give up personal time for lesson preparation, marking homework, meetings, talking to parents and many more.

b Rewrite the paragraph in **5a**, correcting the mistakes you underlined.

Stage 4: Writing a final draft

> Not every person who wants to be a teacher should become one.

6 **a** Imagine that your employer or place of study has asked you to write an article giving advice to people considering your own career or course of study. Think of ideas and then put them in a logical order.

ideas	order
•	☐
•	☐
•	☐

b Write your article.
- Write a first draft using your notes in **6a**.
- Read your first draft and check for mistakes.
- Write the final draft of your article.
- Give your article to your teacher next class.

Tick the things you can do in English in the Reading and Writing Progress Portfolio, p88.

Reading and Writing Portfolio 2

Letters to a newspaper

Reading two letters to a newspaper
Writing giving emphasis
Review habits in the present and past; comparative forms

1 Read both letters quickly. Which statement do they <u>both</u> agree with?

a Schools don't spend enough time teaching speaking and listening.
b Parents don't spend enough time talking and listening to their children.
c Children are more interested in technology than reading and writing.

A

Why isn't more being done to deal with the problem of 'screen bingeing', which we feel strongly is the real cause of so much illiteracy among kids?

In our research, we found a new generation of children who are spending an average of 7.5 hours a day in front of the computer or TV. More and more often, they are doing this alone in their bedrooms or on a portable screen; even if they're among people, they're only paying attention to their laptop. In many homes the family unit has completely broken down, with kids having no basic communication skills at all. This is obviously having a big impact on how they learn to read and write.

It's time we stopped blaming the school system and looked again at how we are bringing up our kids. Having a conversation with them from time to time would help! And it is also time for the government to take the issue of 'screen bingeing' very seriously indeed. Poor literacy is only one of the many problems caused by kids spending far too much time in front of the TV or computer screen.

There is a place for modern media, but like a lot of good things in life, we need a healthy balance.

TERESA ORANGE
LOUISE O'FLYNN
Authors
The Media Diet for Kids
London SW6

B

A lot of people seem to blame absolutely everything that goes wrong on the media, as Teresa Orange and Louise O'Flynn do (Letters, 3rd March). And yet a huge amount of our school homework requires us to use the Internet for research. We learn a lot from television, and you can too, if you are selective. Computer games are supposed to be good for developing your brain. And some of my best discussions with friends have been about computer games or television programmes.

If parents want children to improve their communication skills, perhaps they should communicate more themselves! My own parents are so busy these days that more often than not we don't even eat together as a family – we just eat fast food in front of the TV, often in separate rooms. Not much chance of a conversation there!

Another reason why so many younger people don't communicate very well is perhaps because schools don't attach enough importance to speaking and listening. From a very early age, probably because of exam pressure, kids are made to focus on reading and writing.

Time does move on and technology isn't going to just go away. Perhaps parents and schools should move on too, and appreciate modern media, while at the same time finding the time to have proper conversations with their children!

SALLY PORTER (16)
Birmingham

2 Read the letters again. Are these statements true (T) or false (F)?

In Letter A, the writers:

1 [T] feel that most children spend too long in front of a screen.
2 [ ] think that a lot of parents and children no longer talk to each other.
3 [ ] believe that schools should be responsible for teaching children to communicate.
4 [ ] would like to ban computers and television.

In Letter B, the writer:

5 [ ] believes that children get a lot of benefit from the media.
6 [ ] partly blames TV for the lack of conversation at home.
7 [ ] thinks that schools don't spend enough time on reading and writing.
8 [ ] points out that adults should learn to accept new technology.

HELP WITH WRITING
Giving emphasis

3 a The letter writers use many words and phrases to give emphasis to their opinions. Fill in the gaps in sentences 1–12 with the words in the boxes, to emphasise the phrases in bold.

LETTER A

| ~~strongly~~ completely far so much |
| at all indeed More and more only |

1 … which we feel _strongly_ is the real cause of _____ **illiteracy** among kids?

2 _____ **often** they are doing this alone …

3 … the family unit has _____ **broken down** …

4 … **no basic communication skills** _____ .

5 … **very seriously** _____ .

6 Poor literacy is _____ **one** of the many problems caused by kids spending _____ **too much** time …

LETTER B

| even absolutely just |
| huge themselves does |

7 A lot of people seem to blame _____ **everything** that goes wrong …

8 … a _____ **amount** of our school homework …

9 … perhaps **they** should communicate more _____ !

10 … we **don't** _____ **eat together** …

11 … we _____ **eat** fast food in front of the TV …

12 Time _____ **move on** …

b Which of the words or phrases in **3a** is:

1 only used in negative sentences? _____

2 an auxiliary used to emphasise a verb? _____

3 used to emphasise a pronoun? _____

4 Complete sentences 1–10 with words/phrases from the box to add emphasis.

| ~~absolutely~~ far does strongly at all |
| myself just huge indeed even |

1 I thought _absolutely_ everything he said was true.

2 I didn't agree with the writer's idea _____ .

3 It would be a _____ better idea to ban mobile phones from school altogether.

4 I've had a similar experience _____ .

5 I _____ don't think that fox hunting should be allowed.

6 The government's foreign policy is very short-sighted _____ .

7 Recycling every bit of household rubbish is a _____ commitment for most people.

8 I don't think the writer _____ believes this himself!

9 This issue really _____ need to be discussed.

10 In our neighbourhood, most people feel very _____ that dogs should always be kept on a lead.

5 a Choose one of these topics or your own idea. Make notes in the table.

- Should we ban smoking everywhere, even at home?
- Should all education be free?
- Should cars be banned in city centres?
- Should everyone have to learn at least one foreign language?

topic	
my opinion	
facts and examples	

b Write a letter to a newspaper giving your opinion about the topic you chose.

- Use your notes from **5a**.
- Decide what will be in each paragraph.
- Use some words/phrases from **3** to give emphasis to your opinions.
- Read and check for mistakes.
- Give your letter to your teacher next class.

Tick the things you can do in English in the Reading and Writing Progress Portfolio, p88.

Reading and Writing Portfolio 3

Advice leaflets

Reading a police leaflet about personal safety
Writing leaflets: giving advice
Review conditionals; modals; crime vocabulary

1 Read the leaflet quickly. Choose the best title, a–c.

a Self-defence and the law
b How to avoid being robbed
c Personal safety out and about

The chances of you or a member of your family becoming a victim of violent crime in the UK are low. Violent crimes, such as mugging, by strangers in public places, are still rare and are a very small part of recorded crime.

By taking a few precautions, however, you can make yourself even less likely to become a victim.

Line 7 Many are common sense and might be things that you already do. Making yourself safer doesn't mean changing your entire lifestyle, personality or wardrobe and it doesn't mean never going out at all.

- ¹You will always be safest in bright, well-lit and busy areas. Walk down the middle of the pavement if the street is deserted.
- Try to look and act confident. Look like you know where you are going.
- When out, you shouldn't listen to music loudly with headphones. Stay alert to your surroundings.
- ²If a vehicle suddenly stops alongside you, turn and walk in the other direction – you can turn much faster than a car.
- Try not to be conspicuous about the valuables you are carrying. Do you need to constantly check your smartphone? Are you wearing any obviously expensive jewellery? Thieves notice these things.
- You might like to spread your valuables around your body. For example, keep your phone in your bag, your house keys in your trouser pocket and your money in your jacket.

- If someone tries to take something from you, it may be better to let them take it rather than get into a confrontation and risk injury. ³Shout "fire" rather than "help" – it can get more results.
- You can use reasonable force in self-defence. You are allowed to protect yourself using something you are carrying anyway (for example, keys or a can of deodorant), but you may not carry a weapon.
- If you do decide to defend yourself, be aware that your attacker might be stronger than you or ⁴may take what you are using in self-defence and use it against you. It is often better just to shout loudly and run away.
- ⁵You should always think about how you would act in different situations before you are in them. Would you defend yourself (using reasonable force) and risk further injury? Or would you give an attacker what they want without a fight? Think about the options now because if you were ever attacked, there wouldn't be time.

2 Read the leaflet again. Choose the best answers.

1 The number of violent crimes committed each year in the UK is:
   a increasing.
   b decreasing.
   c not very high. ✓

2 What does *Many* refer to in line 7?
   a the types of crime you might experience
   b the things you can do to prevent attacks
   c criminals who might attack you

3 Which thing does the leaflet not suggest changing?
   a where you walk
   b what you wear
   c what time you go out

4 What does the leaflet advise against?
   a keeping everything in the same bag
   b carrying any valuable items
   c keeping your phone in your pocket

5 If you are attacked, the leaflet advises you:
   a to consider giving attackers what they want.
   b to defend yourself.
   c to use a weapon.

6 You should think about your reaction to an attack now because:
   a they can happen at any time.
   b they happen very often.
   c in an attack, you wouldn't be able to think carefully.

HELP WITH WRITING Leaflets: giving advice

3 Read the leaflet again. Match the underlined sentences to these structures, which are often used to give advice.

> ~~will~~   should   modal verbs of possibility
> zero conditional   imperatives

1 _____will_____   4 _____
2 _____   5 _____
3 _____

4 The writers make their advice softer and more friendly by using certain verbs and phrases. Find sentences in the leaflet that mean the same as sentences a–e.

a Look positive when you are walking.
   Try _to look and act confident._

b Don't use expensive possessions in the street.
   Try _____

c Don't put all your stuff in one pocket.
   You might _____

d Consider giving attackers what they want.
   … it _____

e The criminal will possibly be more physically powerful than you are.
   … be _____

5 Here is some advice from a leaflet on security in the home. Rewrite each point using the word in brackets.

1 Have your keys in your hand when you approach your home. (try) _Try to have your keys in your hand when you approach your home._

2 Do you have a security system? Think about installing one. (if) _____

3 Keep a list of phone numbers you might need in an emergency. (try) _____

4 Consider installing a light outside your home. (might) _____

5 It's a good idea to ask a neighbour to look after your house when you're on holiday. (should) _____

6 It's a bad idea to leave spare keys outside the house. (don't) _____

7 Is there someone in your house? Go to a neighbour and call the police. (if) _____

8 If you see signs of a break-in, remember that someone could still be in your house. (aware) _____

6 Sentences 1–5 are from different leaflets. Match them to titles a–e.

1 You may feel more comfortable carrying a phone with you in case of breakdown. _a_
2 If you chat to the driver, be careful not to give out any personal details. ____
3 Don't give personal information like your email address to strangers. ____
4 Be aware that it can be difficult for motorists to see you. Use lights when it gets dark. ____
5 Try to find out which vaccinations you might need at least six weeks before you fly. ____

a ~~Personal safety: cars~~
b Travelling abroad: safety tips
c Safety online for children
d Safety when cycling
e Using taxis or minicabs

7 Write a leaflet giving advice using one of the titles a–e in **6** or your own idea.

- Include an introduction.
- Use the structures and phrases in **3** and **4**.
- Read and check for mistakes.
- Give your leaflet to your teacher next class.

> Tick the things you can do in English in the Reading and Writing Progress Portfolio, p88.

Reading and Writing Portfolio 4

A biography

Reading a biography of Johnny Depp
Writing a short biography: avoiding repetition; adding detail and personal comment
Review narrative verb forms, connectors, relative clauses

1 Read the article about Johnny Depp quickly. Match topics 1–5 to paragraphs A–E.

1 His successful films _D_
2 His early life _____
3 His home life _____
4 His musical beginnings _____
5 His early acting career _____

 A RELUCTANT STAR

A One of Hollywood's top actors, Johnny Depp has followed an unusual road to stardom. Born in Kentucky in 1963 to a family with Cherokee ancestry, **they** lived in 20 different places before eventually settling in Florida, when Johnny was nine. A teenage rebel, **he** dropped out of school at 15 because of **his** unhappiness following his parents' divorce.

B Over the next few years, Depp played guitar for several garage bands, achieving some local success with **one** called The Kids. **The band** relocated to Los Angeles in search of a record deal. <u>Unfortunately</u>, they struggled to survive in **such a competitive environment** and Depp had to do a variety of jobs, including selling pens. It was while he was **there** that Depp, at 20, married Lori Anne Allison, **who** introduced him to **her** actor friend, Nicolas Cage. It was Cage who encouraged Depp to take up acting himself.

C Depp, although not keen on **the idea**, <u>reluctantly</u> auditioned for his first film A Nightmare on Elm Street in 1984. The Kids split up soon after the release of **the movie** and Depp got other small parts. However, it was the TV series 21 Jump Street which <u>suddenly</u> made him a teenage idol during the 80s. Embarrassed by **this**, Depp decided that from then on he would only appear in roles which he felt were 'right' for **him**.

D He decided to wait for a more serious role to come along. <u>Luckily</u>, one soon **did**. In 1990 he starred in Edward Scissorhands, **which** brought him the critical acclaim he wanted. He **then** went on to appear in a wide variety of different films, including What's eating Gilbert Grape?, Donnie Brasco, Chocolat and Charlie and the Chocolate Factory. Such films made him popular, but it was his role as Jack Sparrow in the smash hit Pirates of the Caribbean which <u>probably</u> first made him an international star.

E Depp's marriage did not last. In 1998 he met and fell in love with French actress and singer Vanessa Paradis with **whom** he had two children, Lily Rose and Jack, although Depp and Paradis are no longer together. Meanwhile, Depp continues to surprise us with film roles **that** are unusual and interesting.

2 How are these topics connected to Johnny Depp? Complete the sentences.

1 Kentucky
Depp was _born there._

2 The Kids
The name of a _____.

3 Los Angeles
Depp went there to _____.

4 Nicolas Cage
The actor who encouraged _____.

5 A Nightmare on Elm Street
This was the name of Depp's _____.

6 21 Jump Street
This was the name of the TV series which _____.

7 Pirates of the Caribbean
This film made Depp an _____.

8 Lily Rose and Jack
They are _____.

70

HELP WITH WRITING
avoiding repetition; adding detail and personal comment

3 Possessive adjectives, pronouns, adverbs and other words are all used to avoid repeating words and phrases. What do the words in bold in the article refer to?

Paragraph A: they ¹ *Depp's family*
he ² _____ his ³ _____
Paragraph B: one ⁴ _____
the band ⁵ _____ such a competitive environment ⁶ _____
there ⁷ _____ who ⁸ _____
her ⁹ _____
Paragraph C: the idea ¹⁰ _____
the movie ¹¹ _____
this ¹² _____ him ¹³ _____
Paragraph D: did ¹⁴ _____
which ¹⁵ _____ then ¹⁶ _____
Paragraph E: whom ¹⁷ _____
that ¹⁸ _____

4 a The underlined adverbs 1–5 from the article can add detail and personal comment to a piece of factual writing. Match adverbs 1–5 to similar words or expressions a–e.

1 unfortunately *b*
2 reluctantly _____
3 suddenly _____
4 luckily _____
5 probably _____

a unexpectedly
b sadly
c unwillingly
d fortunately
e very likely

b Find the underlined adverbs 1–5 in the article. Which ones are used:

1 at the beginning of the sentence?

_____ , _____

2 before the main verb?

_____ , _____ , _____

5 Replace the word or phrase in bold with one of the words from the box.

| ~~He~~ | this | them | His | one | then | he | did |

1 Anthony Horowitz is the author of *Stormbreaker*.
Anthony Horowitz *He* is a very popular writer.

2 He wrote *Stormbreaker* when he was 50. He wasn't famous until **he was 50.** _____ .

3 The hero of the book is a teenage boy. **The hero's** _____ name is Alex Rider.

4 Alex's uncle dies mysteriously. After **he dies mysteriously** _____ , Alex discovers that **his uncle** _____ used to be a spy.

5 Horowitz has written more books about Alex Rider. There are ten of **the books** _____ altogether.

6 I don't have a copy of the book, but my son has **a copy** _____ .

7 I didn't see the film of *Stormbreaker*, but my son **saw the film** _____ .

6 Choose the best word to complete the sentences.

1 Tiger Woods is (probably)/fortunately still one of the world's greatest golfers.
2 *Unexpectedly/Unfortunately*, I've never had the chance to go to a Madonna concert.
3 Jacqueline Wilson writes books for young people. Amongst girls she is *luckily/very likely* even more popular than JK Rowling.
4 Wayne Rooney is my favourite footballer. *Reluctantly/Sadly*, he is not playing as well as he used to.
5 Jamie Oliver's TV cookery series *unwillingly/suddenly* made him an overnight success.

7 a Think of a person who you admire. It could be a writer, sports person, actor, singer, politician or someone you know. Find out about him/her and make notes in the table.

early life	
personal information	
career achievements	
why you admire him/her	

b Write a short biography of the person.
- Use your notes from **7a**.
- Use words in **3** to avoid repetition.
- Use adverbs to add interest or personal comment. Choose from the ones in **4** as well as others you know.
- Read and check for mistakes.
- Give your biography to your teacher next class.

Tick the things you can do in English in the Reading and Writing Progress Portfolio, p88.

Reading and Writing Portfolio 5

Preparing a presentation

Reading a science presentation
Writing the language of presentations
Review Present Simple for facts

1 Read the presentation notes quickly. Match headings a–e to sections 1–5.

a ~~The power of the sun~~
b The dangers of sunlight
c Summary
d The benefits of sunlight for health
e The importance of sunlight to the world

The Science of Sunshine

What I want to do today is talk to you about the science of sunshine.

1

a The power of the sun

Let me begin by looking at some key facts. The power of the sun is ^{1} __c__ to be 386 billion, billion watts. What this means is that in 15 minutes, the sun produces as ^{2} _____ energy as the world's population uses in a year. And if you're from somewhere with weather like the UK, did you know that a two-week holiday in a ^{3} _____ country gives you the equivalent of a whole year of sun at home?

2

_____
Like me, you probably only think about the sun when you're deciding what to wear in the morning. In fact, the sun is ^{4} _____ essential to almost all life on Earth. Plants use the energy from sunlight to change air into their food, and humans and animals use the sun indirectly by eating plants or plant-eating animals.

3

_____
Now let me turn to some of the main reasons why the sun is good for you. ^{5} _____ we are often told that sunshine is dangerous, recent research shows that sunlight can help to protect you from certain types of cancer. What's more, it provides us with our main source* of vitamin D, which makes our bones stronger. The other main benefit is an emotional one. The sun can change your mood chemically and ^{6} _____ depression.

4

_____
As I said earlier, most of our vitamin D comes from sunshine. However, only ten minutes of sunshine each day gives us all we need. And even in the UK, it can take as little as half an hour to ^{7} _____ sunburnt. The sun's energy reaches us in the form of ultraviolet radiation. And while this gives us a healthy-looking tan, it also causes skin cancer. This disease ^{8} _____ about 50,000 British people every year. ^{9} _____ half of Australians develop the disease in their lifetime.

5

_____
So let me finish by saying that the sun is crucial* to both us and the planet. And we should get ^{10} _____ sunlight each day. However too much sun can be extremely harmful to our health. And we must always make sure we take suitable protection against strong sunlight.

* *source* = the place something comes from
* *crucial* = extremely important or necessary

2 Read the presentation notes again and fill in gaps 1–10 with the best words.

	a	b	c	d
1	guessed	approximately	(c) estimated	roughly
2	great	high	much	many
3	sunshine	sun	sunlight	sunny
4	very	extremely	absolutely	enormously
5	Although	Even	However	Despite
6	avoid	put off	check	prevent
7	catch	get	obtain	find
8	influences	concerns	moves	affects
9	Approximate	Around	Close	Just
10	a little	some of	a few	a bit

72

HELP WITH WRITING
The language of presentations

3 a Read the presentation notes again. Fill in the gaps in these phrases.

1 What I want to do today _is talk to you_ about …
2 Let me _____ at …
3 _____ means is that …
4 … _____ know that … ?
5 Now _____ to …
6 As I _____ , …
7 So let me _____ that …

b Match phrases 1–7 in **3a** to their functions a–g.

a focusing people on the overall subject of the presentation: _1_
b explaining a complicated idea in more detail: ____
c signalling the end of a presentation: ____
d referring to an earlier point: ____
e beginning the first part of the presentation: ____
f asking a question to present an interesting fact: ____
g making your next point: ____

4 a Match presentations titles A–D to sentences 1–8. Use each title twice.

A The science of stars
B The environmentally friendly workplace
C Climate change
D Looking after unusual animals at home

1 The next thing I'm going to talk about is what kinds are popular.
   _D_
2 I told you a few minutes ago that the temperature of the Earth will increase by up to 6°C in the next 100 years. ____
3 One interesting fact is that leaving ten computers on overnight for a year costs £1,000. ____
4 This morning, I'm going to talk to you about keeping exotic pets. ____
5 The nearest solar system to Earth is over four light years away, which means that we are seeing what it looked like four years ago. ____
6 Now I'm going to tell you how you can save energy in your office. ____
7 The first thing I'm going to talk about is how stars are born. ____
8 In conclusion, I'd like to tell you what we can do about this worrying global problem. ____

b Complete sentences 1–8 so that they mean the same as sentences 1–8 in **4a**. Use the phrases in **3a**.

1 Now _let me turn to_ what kinds of exotic pet are popular.
2 As _____ , the temperature of the Earth will increase by up to 6°C in the next 100 years.
3 Did you _____ ten computers on overnight for a year costs £1,000?
4 What I _____ keeping exotic pets.
5 The nearest solar system to Earth is over four light years away. What this _____ are seeing what it looked like four years ago.
6 Now let _____ how you can save energy in your office.
7 Let me _____ how stars are born.
8 So let _____ what we can do about this worrying global problem.

5 a Choose one of the titles in **4a** or think of an idea for a presentation about your own work or studies. Make notes in the table.

title of presentation	
different sections of the presentation	
interesting facts	
useful phrases	

b Write your presentation.
- Use your notes in **5a**.
- Use the language of presentations in **3a**.
- Read and check for mistakes.
- Give your presentation to your teacher next class.

Tick the things you can do in English in the Reading and Writing Progress Portfolio, p88.

Reading and Writing Portfolio 6

Describing a place you love

Reading a description of a place
Writing describing places: reduced relative clauses, strong adjectives
Review travel and tourism

1 Read this description of a town in Turkey and match topics 1–5 to paragraphs A–E.

1 codes and customs   2 the wildlife   3 places to visit   4 the town   5 where Dalyan is
  c   _____   _____   _____   _____

A town I love

A The <u>tiny</u> town of Dalyan is in south-west Turkey, about 25 kilometres from Dalaman airport. This pretty village is situated away from the coast in a peaceful river setting, **overlooked** by pine-covered hills and dramatic 4th-century rock tombs **carved** into the cliffs.

B Dalyan is the perfect place to unwind and relax and there are some <u>amazing</u> restaurants on the riverfront. I particularly look forward to sitting outside eating the <u>delicious</u> fish caught in the lake that same day. There's also a wide variety of <u>fascinating</u> shops and a small market, where I enjoy looking for presents: soap **made** from olive oil, the traditional Turkish good luck 'eye', **supposed to** protect you from evil, or even a beautiful handmade carpet.

C A custom which many visitors enjoy is bargaining over prices. The locals are <u>delighted</u> when you bargain with them and you will often end up paying less than half of what you were originally told. Try to respect other customs, though, by remembering not to point, or blow your nose. If you are taken to visit a mosque, remember to cover your shoulders and remove your shoes before going in.

D The whole area is one of <u>outstanding</u> beauty and Dalyan provides a <u>unique</u> natural environment due to the mixture of salt water from the Mediterranean Sea and fresh water from Koycegiz Lake. Because of this, it is home to <u>vast</u> numbers of fish and other waterlife as well as the birds of various species – many of which are not found elsewhere in the world – which feed on them. Dalyan is also famous as one of the last remaining homes of the endangered Caretta Mediterranean turtles, which return to Iztuzu beach every year between May and September to lay their eggs.

E The beach is famous for its fine sand, shallow turquoise sea and non-stop sunshine. It's the ideal seaside spot, **reached** by a short boat or bus ride from Dalyan, through <u>spectacular</u> scenery. Local fishermen take visitors to see the surrounding sights. Those in search of history can be rowed across the river and walk up to the ancient Greek city of Kaunos, past the rock tombs to the <u>ancient</u> theatre, baths and temples. People **interested** in looking younger can take a boat trip to the hot springs and mud baths, **said** to contain anti-ageing properties. Nature lovers can go bird-watching on Koycegiz Lake, **best done** in the early morning. You can have great fun in Dalyan, but in the end what makes it a place that I return to over and over again is the warmth and friendliness of the people who live there.

2 Read the description again and complete the sentences.

1 Dalyan's situation is attractive because of its _peaceful_ setting on the _____, its hills covered by _____ trees and the tombs carved into the _____.
2 The writer likes eating _____ in the local restaurants and looking for _____ to take home.
3 You will pay less when you are shopping if you do as the locals do and _____ with them over the prices.
4 A lot of rare _____ are found in Dalyan because they feed off the waterlife.
5 The local people are _____ and _____.

HELP WITH WRITING
Describing places: reduced relative clauses, strong adjectives

3 Look at the words in bold in the article. Add words to the sentences to make relative clauses.

1. … in a peaceful river setting, (_which/that is_) overlooked by …
2. … rock tombs (_____) carved into the cliffs.
3. … soap (_____) made from olive oil.
4. … the good luck 'eye', (_____) supposed to protect you …
5. … the ideal seaside spot, (_____) reached by …
6. People (_____) interested in looking younger…
7. … the hot springs and mud baths, (_____) said to contain …
8. … bird-watching on Koycegiz Lake, (_____) best done …

4 Match the 'strong' descriptive adjectives <u>underlined</u> in the article to these phrases.

1. very nice/good   _amazing_
2. very big (numbers) _____
3. very old _____
4. very interesting _____
5. very impressive (scenery) _____
6. very small _____
7. very special/exceptional _____
8. very tasty _____
9. very happy _____
10. very rare/the only one _____

5 Join these sentences together, using a present or past participle.

1. Dalyan is a tiny town. It's located between Marmaris and Fethiye.
   Dalyan is a tiny town located between Marmaris and Fethiye.
2. We crossed the river in a small boat. It was rowed by a man from Dalyan.
3. I saw a turtle. It was swimming in the lake.
4. Kaunos was an important Greek town. It was founded in the 6th century BC.
5. We went for a boat trip. It was organised by the tour company.
6. The Turkish 'eye' is a good-luck charm. It is seen everywhere in the town.
7. I took a photo of my wife. She was bargaining for carpets.

6 Replace the words in bold in the email below with words from **4**.

      an amazing

Having ¹**a very good** time here – driving for hours every day, in ²**a very old** car (must be 30 years old!) we have hired. I hope it doesn't break down before we get back! There has been some really ³**impressive** scenery to look at. In the evenings, we've been stopping at restaurants and eating some ⁴**very tasty** seafood. Bill and Jen were ⁵**very happy** to see us, but their house is ⁶**very small**, so we're staying in a hotel. Went to a ⁷**very interesting** museum yesterday – will tell you all about it soon.

7 a Think of a place you love and make notes for a magazine article about it.

name of the place	
where it is	
its natural features	
what there is to do and see	
why it's so special	

b Write your article.
- Use your notes from **7a**.
- Decide what you will include in each paragraph.
- Use relative clauses and reduced relative clauses.
- Use adjectives from **4**.
- Give your article to your teacher next class.

> Tick the things you can do in English in the Reading and Writing Progress Portfolio, p88.

Reading and Writing Portfolio 7

Including relevant information

Reading a leaflet, an article, an email, notes and a fundraising letter
Writing semi-formal letters/emails: including relevant information
Review verb forms

1 Read A–D. Write the missing information 1–10 in email E.

A

CHARITY CYCLE RIDE

Come and cycle from Land's End to John O'Groats for the charity of your choice. During March and April, we will be organising groups to make the incredible 1,400-kilometre journey from the south-west corner of England to the north-west tip of Scotland. If you're

B

Last updated 12.41

Ambitious plans for Four Walls?

THE CHARITY Four Walls' target this year is an ambitious one: £20 million. That's a 33% increase over last year's £15 million. This is significant given that Four

C

From: Four Walls fundraising [funds@fourwalls.org]
To: Huw Price [hprice@mailme.com]
Subject: Your charity cycle ride
Attachment: Fourwallsprofile.pdf

Dear Huw,

Thank you for your email about your cycle ride. I am happy to attach some background information on the charity.

We wish you good luck on 2nd April!

Yours sincerely,
Anya Noakes
Publicity Department

Four Walls — Since 2001

D

Charity cycle ride

- *Leave home on 2nd April, midday, for Land's End*
- *How long? Less than ten days!*
- *New bike?*
- *Set up blog at huw-lejog.com*
- *Write letters – ask for £10?*

E

Dear Thomas,

On ¹ _2nd April_ I will be beginning my ² _____ kilometre cycle ride from ³ _____ to John O'Groats in support of Four Walls, the charity for homeless children in Britain.

Over one million children live in bad housing in Britain. That's enough to fill the cities of Edinburgh, Bath and Manchester. These children are living in damp, cold and infested flats and houses often poorly maintained by landlords. Or they are homeless, waiting in emergency housing for a permanent home.

Four Walls was only set up in ⁴ _____ , but with the ⁵ _____ raised last year, Four Walls helped 14,312 children to get back into a home. In the year ahead, Four Walls is aiming at increasing that total by ⁶ _____ , to ⁷ _____ .

I am asking each person who gets this letter to sponsor me for my ride. If you can help by giving ⁸ _____ , that would be less than 1p per kilometre that I cycle! But if you can't afford that, any amount would be welcome.

Thanks so much for reading this email. It means a lot to me and much more to the children who Four Walls helps every year. Do send me an email at ⁹ _____ if you'd like more information about my ride or Four Walls. And do come along to wave me goodbye from my house when I leave on the ¹⁰ _____ at midday.

Yours,
Huw

PS I'll be updating my blog throughout the journey so check out www.huw-lejog.com from April.

HELP WITH WRITING
Semi-formal letters/emails: including relevant information

2 Read Huw's fundraising email again. Which information does it contain?

1 his email address ✓
2 the postal address of the charity Four Walls
3 how to follow the progress of his ride
4 who he will be riding with
5 what the charity does
6 where he is cycling
7 what made him decide to do the ride
8 the amount he would like people to give

3 Look at these other types of letter/email. Cross out two things that you don't need to include in each letter.

1 A letter/email of complaint:
   a ~~a PS~~
   b what you would like done about the complaint
   c a description of the situation you are complaining about
   d your bank account details

2 A job application:
   a why you are interested in the job
   b how much money you want
   c why you are suitable for the job
   d a list of all the times you are available for interview

3 A letter/email asking for more information from a language school:
   a the areas of grammar you find most difficult
   b where you saw the advertisement
   c a list of the English books you've read
   d your current level of English

4 a Read the email. There are five pieces of information that are not necessary. Underline them and number them 1–5.

Dear Ms. Turnbull,

Thank you for your request for information on our pottery course (1) in response to the advertisement in *The Post*. This year the course will be running on Tuesdays, from 7.30 to 9.30 p.m., beginning on 13th September. Last year's course was on Mondays.

We have very low fees for the course. To book your course, please send us a cheque for £20 as a deposit. The fees will be increasing next year.

You may bring your own tools, but necessary items are provided.

You also enquired about parking at the College. There is a large car park, but it is often full until 5.00 p.m.

Yours sincerely
Jenny Parks

---

b Jenny does not include some important details in her email. Replace the phrases you underlined in **4a** with phrases a–e below.

		replaces
a	at Camden College, Morley Road.	(1)
b	which is opposite the college on Morley Rd.	
c	Please make cheques payable to Camden College.	
d	The total fee for the course is £120.	
e	The course will last for ten weeks.	

5 a Choose one of these situations. Make notes in the table.

- You have decided to raise some money for a local charity by doing a marathon. Write a fundraising letter to people explaining exactly what you are doing, when you are doing it, what the charity is, who it helps and asking them for their donations.
- A foreign friend is staying with you for a few days next month. Write an email saying what you have planned to do and why, what they should bring, and describing arrangements for picking them up when they arrive.

points to include	order of the information

b Write your letter or email.
- Use your notes in **5a**.
- Check that you have included all necessary information in your notes.
- Check you haven't included any unnecessary information.
- Read and check for mistakes.
- Give your letter or email to your teacher next class.

> Tick the things you can do in English in the Reading and Writing Progress Portfolio, p88.

Reading and Writing Portfolio 8

Reporting facts

Reading an article reporting on consumer spending
Writing generalising; giving examples
Review the passive; comparatives

1 Read the report quickly. Complete the sentence.

These days, people are spending their money on:

a things they can't afford.
b unnecessary luxuries.
c key household items.

Hard times

According to a recent survey, more than 80% of the population in Britain have changed their spending habits over the last year as the cost of living has shot up, people's pay has been frozen and many have lost their jobs. As a result of the recession*, over half (51%) of the population appear to be buying fewer non-essentials **such as** clothes and DVDs. Close to half of consumers say that they now tend to shop around before buying goods, with over a fifth admitting that they have started to buy non-essentials from supermarkets rather than independent shops. "People are uncertain about what the future holds financially, and the most natural response is to be cautious," says the author of the report. "As we see households looking for ways to reduce monthly out-goings, non-essentials are the first to go. However, for those who do not wish to go without their non-essentials, the supermarket chains seem to offer a better deal."

Generally speaking, it is women who tend to be leading the way when it comes to cutting costs. More women than men have switched to 'value' brands or have started using vouchers when shopping. And **in the main,** it is women who are far more likely to set themselves a budget and keep to it.

The recession has also had a major impact on UK leisure habits. Even before the recession, almost a quarter of the population said that they were happy to stay in more often because of in-home entertainment technology. The recession seems to be accelerating this trend, with 53% of consumers staying in more and 59% spending less when they do go out. **On the whole,** when people go out to eat they tend to look for good deals, order cheaper dishes and perhaps skip dessert.

There is no doubt that times are difficult. But despite – or maybe because of – economic stress, people aren't totally giving up on treats. It's not about luxuries, though, but simpler, less costly ways of finding comfort, **like** eating sweets and chocolate. "People are looking for a quick fix. Old-fashioned sweets are particularly popular because you go back to your childhood memories," says the researcher.

In his view, this is the best way to increase happiness – making a series of smaller purchases rather than one big one. For example, he believes that people who go to several concerts given by local bands appeared to be happier **in most cases** than the people who spent the same amount but got great seats at a concert with a top band.

* recession = a time when the economy of a country is not successful

2 Read the report again and answer the questions.

1 Why have people started buying fewer luxuries?
   Because they have less money to spend.

2 What examples are given of luxury goods?

3 Why are more people shopping in supermarkets?

4 What three things do women do to save money on their shopping?

5 What change in free-time activities had already begun before the recession?

6 Give two reasons why sweet treats have become more popular.

7 How can you go out more but not spend more, according to a researcher?

HELP WITH WRITING
Generalising; giving examples

3 **a** Look at the sentences. Circle the phrases used in the article.

1 Over half of the population *are buying/appear to be buying* fewer non-essentials …
2 the supermarket chains *offer/seem to offer* a better deal.
3 … it is women who *tend to be leading/are leading* the way …
4 … (people) *look for/tend to look for* good deals …

b Choose the correct phrase.

a The phrases *seem* and *appear to* make generalisations sound *more/less* certain.
b The phrase *tend to* emphasises that a generalisation is *always true/not always true*.

4 Look at the words and phrases in bold in the article. Match them to 1–3.

1 phrases which generalise

    on the whole , _____ ,

    _____ , _____

2 words or phrases which come before examples

    _____ , _____

3 words or phrases emphasising that an opinion belongs to a particular person or group

    _____ , _____

5 Change the words and phrases in bold using the words in brackets.

1 The majority of people today **shop** in supermarkets. (seem)

    seem to shop

2 Fewer customers **are buying** organic vegetables. (appear)

    _____

3 Old-fashioned sweets **are getting** increasingly popular. (seem)

    _____

4 Small independent shops **suffer** when a supermarket opens. (tend)

    _____

5 People **are not spending** so much. (appear)

    _____

6 Organic food **is** more expensive. (tends)

    _____

6 Fill in the gaps with these words.

| ~~to~~ | tends | like | whole | generally |
| such | seem | Apparently | main | |

According ^{1} *to* research, the average take-home salary ^{2}_____ to be lower than it used to be. ^{3}_____ speaking, though, increasing numbers of people are choosing to spend their money on enjoying themselves rather than buying goods. ^{4}_____ , 'once in a lifetime' activities ^{5}_____ parachuting or sports car racing have become very popular. On the ^{6}_____ , fewer people are saving money in banks, as the rate of interest is very low. In the ^{7}_____ , too, people ^{8}_____ to be choosing shorter holidays ^{9}_____ as weekend city breaks rather than the traditional two weeks in the summer.

7 **a** Choose one of these ideas. Make notes in the table.

- Write a report for your local newspaper on how public transport facilities in your area could be improved.
- Write a report for your local council saying how shopping, eating or leisure facilities in your town could be improved for the majority of residents.
- Write a report for a college magazine saying what most people of your age group choose to spend their money on.

what the problem is	
how you did your research	
what you suggest doing	
possible results	

b Write your report.

- Use your notes in **7a**.
- Use phrases in **3** and **4** to make generalisations and to make statements less certain where appropriate.
- Read and check for mistakes.
- Give your report to your teacher next class.

Tick the things you can do in English in the Reading and Writing Progress Portfolio, p88.

Reading and Writing Portfolio 9

Website reviews

Reading a review of two websites
Writing reviews: beginning reviews, useful phrases
Review the Internet

1 Read the reviews quickly. Write R (Reddit.com), W (Wikipedia.org) or B (both).

Which website:
a allows readers to vote on its content? ___
b has video? ___
c is multilingual? ___

2 Read the reviews again. Are the sentences true (T), false (F) or the reviews don't say (DS)?

1 [F] Reddit is only for people interested in news.
2 [ ] Reddit was the first website to use the idea of 'voting' for the best story.
3 [ ] 'Subreddits' are a way of organising posts you might be interested in.
4 [ ] The reviewer thinks that Reddit can be a waste of time.
5 [ ] The reviewer of Wikipedia uses it for his or her homework.
6 [ ] You can add information to any article on Wikipedia.
7 [ ] The users of Wikipedia deal with problems like vandalism.
8 [ ] Wikipedia is more accurate than other encyclopedias.

A

Have you ever thought about what it is that makes you read some news articles and not others? Basically, the more prominent the story, the more likely you are to read it. And who decides what is on the front page of a newspaper or the top story on a website? The editor, of course.

Like news websites, [1]Reddit similarly features news from all over the world. But [2]what I love about Reddit is how it collects and displays stories. It is entirely democratic. Anyone can post a question, link, picture or just an observation. If users or 'redditors' like the post, they click a button to recommend it. The more recommendations a post receives, the closer it gets to the front page of the website.

[3]Posts are grouped into different subjects or 'subreddits'. Anyone can start a new subreddit and there are thousands of them. They range from typical subjects such as World News to cute pictures of pets! Users build their own front page on the website by choosing the subreddits they are interested in.

[4]A downside to Reddit is that there's almost too much to read. The conversations that follow popular posts can get very long and I often end up skimming through them to the end. After that, it feels like I've done a lot of reading but I haven't learned much.

However, with users from all over the world writing in almost 50 languages, and over two billion visitors a month, there is always something that's interesting to read on Reddit. Beware: it's addictive!

B

WIKIPEDIA The Free Encyclopedia

When I was young, difficult homework questions could only be answered if: a) your parents knew; b) you lived near the library; or c) you were lucky enough to own a set of encyclopedias. I often used c), as long as the subject didn't begin with S, T or U. We'd lost those books.

Then computers and the CD-ROM appeared. Suddenly encyclopedias had sound, videos and much more. Then along came *Wikipedia* – an online encyclopedia with a difference. Firstly, Wikipedia is huge. The number of articles is around 20 million and it is published in over 280 languages.

And, if you can't find the article you want, you can write it yourself. That's right: anyone can edit existing articles or add a new one!

[5]One of the drawbacks of this fantastic idea is that articles can suffer from vandalism. So controversial topics are 'locked' from editing and any problems are efficiently dealt with by the 650,000 registered 'Wikipedians'. [6]The website is very easy to navigate, with numerous hyperlinks from each article to many others. [7]Additional features include photos, sound and film clips with some articles. But [8]one of the main strengths of Wikipedia is the range and relevance of the content. There are thousands of articles that you wouldn't usually see in encyclopedias and they are constantly being updated. Wikipedia is an incredible resource for everyone ... by anyone!

HELP WITH WRITING
Reviews: beginning reviews, useful phrases

3 The beginning of a review is important because it encourages people to continue reading. Read the first paragraph of each review again. Which review begins by:

a asking you questions to make you think? _____
b trying to make you laugh? _____

4 Fill in the gaps with underlined phrases 1–8 in the reviews.

a saying what the website contains

  Reddit (similarly) features _____

b saying how the website is organised

  _____

  _____

c the good points about a website

  _____

  _____

d the bad points about a website

  _____

  _____

5 Read the beginnings of reviews 1–4. Which one:

a tries to interest you by making a comparison? _3_
b tries to surprise you? _____
c uses the plot of the story to interest you? _____
d is extremely critical? _____

1 In last night's *EastEnders* (BBC 1) Kevin finally died. Rather than moving, the episode was ridiculously sentimental and about as realistic as the chances of me appearing on the show.

2 Four hours long, with an unknown cast and a depressing plot about poor teenage criminals in poor areas of South America, *La Trampa* (The Trap) does not sound gripping. But it is. In fact, it's the most memorable film I've seen in over ten years.

3 Move over Potter, children want to read about the future now. And Suzanne Collin's third instalment of the Hunger Games trilogy, *Mockingjay*, should keep them happy.

4 *Fixation* (The National Theatre, July–September) is a scary tale of a woman whose obsession with a pop star takes over her life and eventually leads her to commit a crime she can never forget.

6 Complete sentence b so that it means the same as a. Use between two and five words, including the word in brackets.

1 a It also has free anti-virus software.
  b _Additional features include_ free anti-virus software. (features)

2 a The accuracy of Google is one of its greatest advantages.
  b _____ of Google is its accuracy. (strengths)

3 a There are two sections on the website.
  b The website _____. (grouped)

4 a These are some of the best graphics I have seen in this game.
  b This _____ of the best graphics I have seen. (features)

5 a It's quite hard to find your way around the site.
  b The site _____. (navigate)

6 a The fuel consumption of this car is a problem.
  b _____ this car is its fuel consumption. (drawbacks)

7 a I love this mobile because of its size.
  b _____ about this mobile is its size. (what)

8 a One thing that isn't good about working at home is not seeing many people.
  b _____ working at home is not seeing many people. (downside)

7 a Think about a website you know and make notes.

what it is	
the content	
what's good and bad about it	
how the site is organised	

b Write a review of the website.
- Use your notes in **7a**.
- Choose a suitable type of beginning from **3** and **5**.
- Use phrases from **4** where appropriate.
- Read and check for mistakes.
- Give your review to your teacher next class.

> Tick the things you can do in English in the Reading and Writing Progress Portfolio, p88.

Reading and Writing Portfolio 10

A discursive article

Reading an article about combining parenthood and careers
Writing a discursive article: common connecting words
Review connecting words

1 Read the article. Where does this paragraph go in the article?

> Working harder and longer, just to end up poorer, is making a lot of fathers think they should be prioritising their quality of life. In other words, doing a lot more of what they want to do. And top of the wish list – for 79% of working fathers – is spending more time with their children.

2 Read the article again and choose the best answers.

1. The writer's system of childcare usually goes wrong
   a. when something unexpected happens. *(circled)*
   b. because of his wife.
   c. because of his children.

2. Why does the writer think that most working fathers are worse off than him?
   a. Because they earn less money.
   b. Because their employers aren't as understanding.
   c. Because they have to work harder than he does.

3. Chris Prince was able to take time off work because
   a. he works freelance.
   b. he got money when he was made redundant.
   c. his wife went back to work.

4. The writer thinks that becoming a full-time father
   a. is a good option.
   b. isn't a practical option.
   c. is financially impossible for everyone.

5. According to the writer, what are the problems of going part-time?
   a. financial difficulties
   b. damage to your career
   c. both a) and b)

The childcare *choice*

A
I am part of a dual-income family. That's right, both my wife and I have jobs. We also have children. We work at different times and everything depends on 'handover'. This works fine ¹**unless anything** interrupts the routine. Excuses for being late that begin with "My wife had to …" don't impress. ²**So** I am always grateful for having an understanding employer.

B
I suspect that many are not so generous. And looking at the current generation of fathers, the future is no better. ³**Despite** missing their children growing up, by 40, their salaries will be peaking* as they begin to be replaced by young graduates. And ⁴**along with** this approaching pay cut comes the news that the government intends to increase the retirement age to 68.

C
Some men can take time off work, usually ⁵**as a result of** a good redundancy package. New father Chris Prince took this option, but he is hoping to pick up a little freelance work over the next year. But if someone isn't offering you some money to leave your job, then what other options are there?

D
You could swap roles. Mother becomes the breadwinner* and father becomes a full-time parent. But this still leaves one of you facing an eight-hour day and then childcare at home – a good recipe for trouble. ⁶**What's more**, it might leave some people with the problem of only one income.

E
⁷**On the other hand**, you could go part-time. Obviously, you're going to take a pay cut. And there are other problems too: "I've noticed myself working on my days off, getting up early so I can put in a few hours at the office before everyone else wakes up," says John Dorian, father of two and part-time web designer.

F
John believes he has a considerate employer and his career won't suffer for his choice, ⁸**although** the evidence from women is not encouraging. A woman who has worked part-time for just a year suffers a 10% long-term reduction in earnings.

G
Personally, my wife and I aren't about to change our system. We know it's not perfect, but it (usually) works. We know we're sometimes too tired to do our best with our children. But we're good parents. Promise.

* *peaking* = reaching their highest point
* *breadwinner* = the person who gets most of the family's income

82

HELP WITH WRITING Common connecting words

3 Read the article again. Replace each word/phrase in bold with a word in the box.

> ~~as long as (nothing)~~   though   Alternatively   Therefore
> as well as   because of   In spite of   Moreover

1 unless (anything) _as long as (nothing)_
2 So _____
3 Despite _____
4 along with _____
5 as a result of _____
6 What's more _____
7 On the other hand _____
8 although _____

4 Complete the table with the pairs of words/phrases in **3**.

condition	addition	cause/effect	contrast
1 _unless_, _as long as_	in addition to, 2 _____	due to, 4 _____	6 _____,
	Furthermore, 3 _____	Consequently, 5 _____	As an alternative, 7 _____,
			even though, 8 _____,

5 Rewrite the sentences using the correct word/phrase.

1 My father was the breadwinner in our family. That meant I saw less of him than my mother.

   a though   b in addition to   (c) consequently

   My father was the breadwinner in our family. Consequently, I saw less of him than my mother.

2 He finds it difficult to get by. It's surprising, because he works full-time.

   a on the other hand   b unless   c despite

3 More women in Britain are having children later in their lives. The reason for this is often their careers.

   a although   b because of   c moreover

4 You could put in the burglar alarm yourself. Or you could have it installed by a professional.

   a alternatively   b even though   c along with

5 All the fathers I know work full-time. In fact, many of them work over 45 hours per week.

   a so   b what's more   c as an alternative

6 She looked after the children. She also worked full-time.

   a due to   b therefore   c as well as

6 a A local newspaper is running a competition. Choose one of these articles. Make notes in the table.

- A year off: what would you do? If you've recently taken or are planning to take at least 12 months off work or studying to do something different, tell us about it.
- We're looking for couples with interesting routines. Write to us and tell us what's unusual about you and your partner's day-to-day life.
- How do you and you partner share household tasks? Has it always been like this? How do you feel about it?

introduction	
main points	
conclusion	

b Write your article.

- Use your notes in **6a**.
- Write your first draft.
- Read your draft and find ways to link your ideas using the connecting words in **4**.
- Write your final draft.
- Read and check for mistakes.
- Give your article to your teacher next class.

> Tick the things you can do in English in the Reading and Writing Progress Portfolio, p88.

Reading and Writing Portfolio 11

Formal and informal emails

Reading two emails asking for and giving information
Writing making arrangements in informal and more formal emails
Review indirect questions; future verb forms; past verb forms

1 a Which email (A or B) is making arrangements for:
1 a business trip? _____
2 a party? _____

b Both emails have four paragraphs and are organised in the same way. Put parts a–d in the order 1–4 in which they occur in the emails.

a _1_ reason for writing
b ____ conclusion
c ____ giving information
d ____ requesting information

A Hi Helen!

Got your invite today – we'd both LOVE to come and help you celebrate your 21st. Thanks very much.

Phil has got a couple of private students at home until about 12 and the traffic leaving our area of London is always a nightmare at that time on a Saturday, so we may well miss the barbecue, worse luck. Anyway, we hope to be turning up some time around 4, if that's OK – I'll give you a buzz when I know the exact time.

Which reminds me, you'll have to tell us how we actually get to your place. I'm fine as far as the motorway turn-off (junction 31?) but after that I haven't a clue where I'm going, so can you text over some directions as our satnav doesn't work any more! Oh, and shall we bring sleeping bags or have you got enough?

Anyway, get in touch if you can think of anything you need. Lots of love, Beth (and Phil) xxxx

PS I've attached some photos!

B Dear Mrs Bannister,

I am writing to thank you for your prompt response regarding my enquiries about accommodation at your apartments.

I received your brochure today. I would like to confirm the provisional booking I made last week for myself and my two colleagues. As I explained in that email, we will be arriving on Sunday evening, 5th October, in time for our conference, which begins on the Monday.

However, I note from your brochure that you only take bookings from Saturday to Saturday. Could you clarify that you will not require payment for Saturday 4th, as we will not be using the apartment? In addition, I would appreciate it if you could let us know what time we will be expected to vacate the apartment on Saturday 11th.

Thank you for your help with these queries. We look forward to meeting you next month and I will shortly be sending a bank transfer for £400 to cover the deposit.

Yours

Fiona Buxton

---

2 Read the emails again. Are these sentences true (T) or false (F)?

1 _F_ Beth and Phil have been invited to a party to celebrate Helen's exam results.
2 ☐ The barbecue is on Saturday evening.
3 ☐ Phil is a teacher.
4 ☐ Beth and Phil are staying overnight at Helen's.
5 ☐ Fiona wants to change the dates of her reservation.
6 ☐ She is going with people from work.
7 ☐ She doesn't want to pay for accommodation on Saturday night.
8 ☐ She would like to have a party in the apartment on the 4th October.
9 ☐ Fiona will send money soon.

HELP WITH WRITING Making arrangements in informal and more formal emails

3 Find formal phrases in email B which mean the same as these phrases.

1 quick reply *prompt response*
2 about my questions _____
3 I got (your brochure) _____
4 I see (from your brochure) _____
5 (Can you) make it clear …? _____
6 (will not) want (payment) _____
7 Also _____
8 We're looking forward (to) _____

4 Are 1–9 usually features of informal English (I) or more formal English (F)?

1 exclamation marks (!) *I*
2 dashes (–) _____
3 missing words (*Got your invite today*) _____
4 direct questions (*Can you email over some directions?*) _____
5 capital letters (*LOVE*) _____
6 adding extra information after the end of the letter (*PS*) _____
7 indirect questions (*I would appreciate it if you could …*) _____
8 specialised language (*regarding*) _____
9 underlining (*a nightmare*) _____

5 Match the informal phrases 1–10 from email A to the more formal phrases a–j.

1	invite	a	have no idea
2	worse luck	b	get in contact
3	turning up	c	would you mind…?
4	give (you) a buzz	d	unfortunately
5	place	e	arriving
6	turn-off	f	would you like us to…?
7	haven't a clue	g	invitation
8	can you …?	h	exit road
9	shall we …?	i	telephone (you)
10	get in touch	j	house

6 Choose the more formal words to complete this email.

Dear Mr Tremayne,
¹*I am writing/Just writing* to confirm that I have ²*received/got* your money transfer and booked your son on our summer activity course. ³*Regarding/About* the ⁴*enquiries/questions* in your letter, ⁵*we don't yet know/we haven't a clue yet* which boys will be sharing a room. ⁶*Also/In addition*, we can't be sure exactly which sports we will be offering, ⁷*worse luck/unfortunately*. ⁸*But/However*, as soon as this is confirmed, I will ⁹*telephone you/give you a buzz*. I would appreciate it if ¹⁰*you would/would you* let me know what time Oscar will be arriving on the 5th.

Yours sincerely,
Jane Pinder

7 a Look at the notes on the invitation and on the language school advert. Choose which email to write and make notes in the table.

Georgie and Colum
are getting married on
Saturday, 6th June
at Newport Registry Office
and would like to invite
___Ruth___
to help them celebrate afterwards.
Reception at 6 p.m.
at the Maze restaurant.

Can I bring Richard?
Are we invited to the actual wedding or just the reception?
Is there parking at the restaurant?

LingoLearners
School of English

- small friendly classes
- accommodation provided
- trips included

www.lingolearners.net

Where are the trips to?
How many students in the class?
Can we stay with host families?
How many hours a day?

informal or more formal?	
what information to give	
what information to ask for	

b Write your email.
- Use your notes from **7a**.
- Use either informal or more formal language.
- Read and check for mistakes.
- Give your email to your teacher next class.

Tick the things you can do in English in the Reading and Writing Progress Portfolio, p88.

Reading and Writing Portfolio 12

A personal email

Reading a personal email about a ghostly experience
Writing a personal email about an experience: common mistakes
Review past verb forms; reported speech

1 Read the email quickly. Is the main purpose to tell Ellie:

  a to do something?
  b about the wedding?
  c about a tour she went on?

2 Read the email again. Are these sentences true (T), false (F) or the email doesn't say (DS)?

1. [F] Sarah and Robin went to Edinburgh to go on a ghost walk.
2. [ ] Sarah didn't think the beginning of the walk was very interesting.
3. [ ] The underground vaults have a reputation for being haunted.
4. [ ] Sarah tried to take a photo of the cobbler.
5. [ ] There was no obvious explanation for the photo Sarah found on her camera.
6. [ ] Members of the company were employed to scare people.
7. [ ] Sarah and Robin both heard strange sounds in the last room.
8. [ ] The guide took Sarah's news seriously.
9. [ ] Fran had seen the cobbler on another visit.
10. [ ] Sarah advised Ellie to go on the tour.

Hi Ellie,

Just couldn't wait to tell you about our trip to Scotland! As you know, it was Sally and George's wedding on the Friday and we weren't getting a train back till Sunday morning so on Saturday night we booked for one of ¹**those 'ghost walks' that Edinburgh is so famous for**.

I wasn't very ²**impressed by** the tour at first – we just walked round the spooky bits of the city, which was OK, I suppose, but things didn't really begin to liven up until we went down into the vaults near South Bridge. Apparently, the BBC said it was 'possibly the most haunted place in Britain' and I can see why!

You go down a stone staircase into these dark damp rooms where families ³**used to live** in the 18th century. Our guide, Fran, told stories about the place ⁴**and said some people had seen a cobbler* working in a corner**. Robin was actually standing there, but he didn't seem to feel anything. Imagine our shock, then, when we looked at the digital pictures ⁵**we'd taken**. Instead of Fran talking to the group we saw the whitish outline of a man, his face quite clear, holding one hand by his ear as if he were listening. There was no movement of air in the room and nothing on the wall, so it ⁶**can't have been a shadow**.

Anyway, we continued our tour and in the last room I ⁷**kept looking** at a particular corner. I had a feeling that a member of the tour company would jump out and scare us. I tried to focus on Fran's ghost story and suddenly I felt a really cold feeling through my right shoulder, up my neck and on my face, but not to my left side, which was warm. I looked over at the corner. Nothing! In the end, I swapped places with Robin, without saying anything to him. Almost immediately, he said he could hear footsteps and he felt like I had. We both got the impression that the spirit was irritated and wanted us to leave. So I told the guide and she cleared the room. Out in the corridor, the coldness disappeared.

On the street, Fran gave us more details of the spirit we had experienced and others we had not. She said ⁸**the tour group** kept records of sightings, including the cobbler and 'ours'. I know you'll be going up there next month, so make sure you go on the tour and tell me if you see anything.

The wedding was great, by the way! The weather was fantastic and Sally looked gorgeous.

Have a good week,

Sarah

*cobbler = someone who mends shoes

HELP WITH WRITING
Common mistakes

3 a Students often make mistakes in language areas a–h when they write. Match the phrases 1–8 in bold in the email to a–h.

a reported speech _4_
b Past Perfect ____
c articles ____
d adjective + preposition ____
e past habit ____
f verb+ing ____
g relative clauses ____
h modal verbs ____

b Match language areas a–h in **3a** with these examples of correct and incorrect sentences.

1 [e] *She used to be my friend.*
       not *She was used to be my friend.*

2 [ ] *I have never believed in ghosts.*
       not *I have never believed in the ghosts.*

3 [ ] *She's terrified of spiders.*
       not *She's terrified with spiders.*

4 [ ] *You should have remembered her birthday.*
       not *You should remembered her birthday.*

5 [ ] *It's the song he wrote about his wife.*
       not *It's the song he wrote it about his wife.*

6 [ ] *I stopped smoking when I had a baby.*
       not *I stopped to smoke when I had a baby.*

7 [ ] *I explained where I had been.*
       not *I explained where I went.*

8 [ ] *She asked me where I was going.*
       not *She asked me where was I going.*

4 Correct four mistakes in each email.

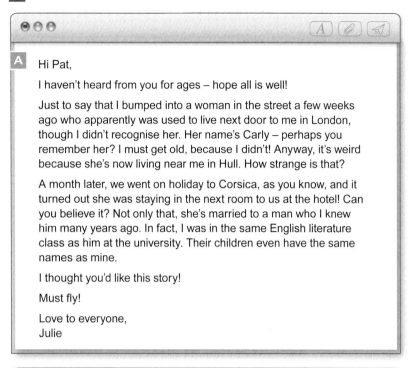

A Hi Pat,

I haven't heard from you for ages – hope all is well!

Just to say that I bumped into a woman in the street a few weeks ago who apparently **was used to live** next door to me in London, though I didn't recognise her. Her name's Carly – perhaps you remember her? I must get old, because I didn't! Anyway, it's weird because she's now living near me in Hull. How strange is that?

A month later, we went on holiday to Corsica, as you know, and it turned out she was staying in the next room to us at the hotel! Can you believe it? Not only that, she's married to a man who I knew him many years ago. In fact, I was in the same English literature class as him at the university. Their children even have the same names as mine.

I thought you'd like this story!

Must fly!

Love to everyone,
Julie

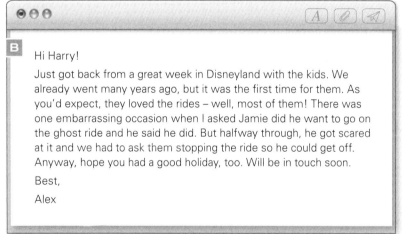

B Hi Harry!

Just got back from a great week in Disneyland with the kids. We already went many years ago, but it was the first time for them. As you'd expect, they loved the rides – well, most of them! There was one embarrassing occasion when I asked Jamie did he want to go on the ghost ride and he said he did. But halfway through, he got scared at it and we had to ask them stopping the ride so he could get off. Anyway, hope you had a good holiday, too. Will be in touch soon.

Best,
Alex

5 a Think about an experience you have had recently and make notes in the table. The experience can be scary, funny, happy or sad.

what happened	
how you felt about it	

b Write an email to a friend and tell them what happened.
- Use your notes in **5a**.
- Read and check for the common mistakes in **3**.
- Write your email again if you need to.
- Give your email to your teacher next class.

> Tick the things you can do in English in the Reading and Writing Progress Portfolio, p88.

Upper Intermediate Reading and Writing Progress Portfolio

Tick the things you can do in English.

Portfolio	Reading	Writing
1 p64	☐ I can understand in detail an article about learning a language.	☐ I can write a detailed article in my own field of interest. ☐ I can plan and draft my writing.
2 p66	☐ I can understand in detail letters in which the writers express their views.	☐ I can write a letter expressing my views and giving reasons. ☐ I can use words and phrases to add emphasis.
3 p68	☐ I can understand in detail a leaflet giving advice.	☐ I can write a leaflet giving advice, using appropriate language.
4 p70	☐ I can read a short biography and understand the development of events.	☐ I can write a short biography giving a detailed description of events and experiences, using appropriate connecting words.
5 p72	☐ I can understand the text of a presentation on a specialised subject.	☐ I can write a detailed presentation on a specialised subject. ☐ I can use appropriate language for sequencing, emphasis and signposting in a presentation.
6 p74	☐ I can read and understand detailed descriptions of places.	☐ I can write a detailed description of a place, using a wide range of descriptive language.
7 p76	☐ I can find, understand and select relevant information from different sources.	☐ I can write a letter or email giving relevant information.
8 p78	☐ I can understand facts, generalisations and opinions in reports.	☐ I can write a report which develops an argument. ☐ I can summarise information from different sources.
9 p80	☐ I can understand a review in detail.	☐ I can write a review of a website.
10 p82	☐ I can understand a writer's point of view in an article.	☐ I can write an article expressing my views. ☐ I can use a wide range of connecting words and phrases.
11 p84	☐ I can understand formal and informal emails.	☐ I can ask for information in a formal or informal email. ☐ I can use a range of informal and more formal language in my writing.
12 p86	☐ I can understand in detail personal emails giving news and expressing feelings.	☐ I can write a personal email giving news and expressing my feelings. ☐ I can correct mistakes in my writing.